EXPLAINING

Explanation is the foundation on which the success or failure of a whole section of teaching can rest. Well done, it saves time and provides motivation. Badly done, it produces chaos.

This book shows what explanation is and what it aims to do. It explores the various strategies open to teachers and by a combination of activities and discussion points it helps them to build up a repertoire of techniques suitable for various situations and to evaluate the effectiveness of their explanations in the classroom. Along the way it covers such issues as the use of an appropriate language register, the place of analogies, building on children's questions and the coping strategies for effective explanation when the teacher herself is unfamiliar with the subject matter.

Ted Wragg is head of the School of Education at Exeter University and the author of many books including *Class Management* and, again with George Brown, *Questioning* in this series. He writes a regular column in the *Times Educational Supplement* and is a frequent commentator for radio and television on education matters.

George Brown is a former lecturer in Education at the University of Nottingham. He too has written many books, including *Effective Teaching in Higher Education* (Routledge 1988).

Clive Carré is coordinator of the Leverhulme Primary Project and series editor for the *Classroom Skills* series. He has taught science at primary and secondary levels and has written and acted as a consultant on science materials in the UK, Australia and Canada.

LEVERHULME PRIMARY PROJECT

The Leverhulme Primary Project, based at Exeter University, directed by Ted Wragg and Neville Bennett and coordinated by Clive Carré is a major survey of primary teacher education since 1988. Its bank of valuable information about what actually happens in classrooms and how teachers are reacting to current changes in education will be used for a variety of publications including the *Classroom Skills* series.

All primary teachers need to master certain basic pedagogical skills. This set of innovative yet practical resource books for teachers covers each of those skills in turn. Each book contains

- Practical, written and oral activities for individual and group use at all stages of professional development
- Transcripts of classroom conversation and teacher feedback and photographs of classroom practice to stimulate discussion
- Succinct and practical explanatory text

Other titles in the series

TALKING AND LEARNING IN GROUPS *Elisabeth Dunne and Neville Bennett*
CLASS MANAGEMENT *E. C. Wragg*
QUESTIONING *George Brown and E. C. Wragg*
EFFECTIVE TEACHING *E. C. Wragg*

Leverhulme Primary Project ■ **Classroom Skills Series**

Series editor
Clive Carré

EXPLAINING

E.C. Wragg and George Brown

London and New York

First published 1993
by Routledge
11 New Fetter Lane, London EC4P 4EE

Simultaneously published in the USA and Canada
by Routledge
29 West 35th Street, New York, NY 10001

© 1993 E.C. Wragg and George Brown
Filmset in Palatino by Selwood Systems, Midsomer Norton
Printed and bound in Great Britain by Butler & Tanner Ltd,
Frome, Somerset

British Library Cataloguing in Publication Data

A catalogue record for this title is available from the British
Library.

Library of Congress Cataloging in Publication Data
Wragg, E. C. (Edward Conrad)
    Explaining/E. C. Wragg and George Brown.
        p.   cm.——(The Leverhulme primary project
classroom skills series)
    Includes bibliographical references and index.
    ISBN 0–415–08387–7
    1. Teaching.   2. Explanation.   I. Brown, George,
    1935–   .
    II. Title.   III. Series.
    LB1027.W65   1993
    371.1'02——dc20   92–19660
                                                              CIP

CONTENTS

PREFACE

Improving the quality of what happens in primary school and preparing children for life in the twenty-first century requires the highest quality of professional training. The Leverhulme Primary Project *Classroom Skills* series and its companion series *Curriculum in Primary Practice* are designed to assist in this training.

The Leverhulme Primary Project *Classroom Skills* series focuses on the essential classroom competences. It explores the classroom strategies available to teachers and the patterns of classroom organization which best assist pupil learning. Throughout, it demonstrates that at the very heart of teacher education is the ability to make sense of what is going on in the classroom. This series of books is based on the research of the Leverhulme Primary Project, a three-year programme of research into various aspects of primary teacher education, funded by the Leverhulme Trust and carried out at the University of Exeter. The companion series, *Curriculum in Primary Practice* helps teachers to make judgements and devise strategies for teaching particular subjects.

Both series are designed to assist teachers at all stages of their professional development. They will be useful for:

- practising teachers
- student teachers
- college and university tutors
- school-based in-service coordinators
- advisory teachers
- school mentors and headteachers.

This book can be used as part of initial training or in in-service programmes in school. The text can also be read by individuals as a source of ideas and it will be helpful in teacher appraisal as an aid to developing professional awareness both for those being appraised and for the appraisers. Like all the books in both series, *Explaining* contains suggested activities which have been tried out by teachers and those in pre-service training and revised in the light of their comments.

We hope that both series will provoke discussion, help you to reflect on your current practice and encourage you to ask questions about everyday classroom events.

Clive Carré
University of Exeter

ACKNOWLEDGEMENTS

My thanks are due to Sarah Crowhurst for her fieldwork on explanations to 8 and 9 year olds, and to Jill Christie who also collected some of the data.

AIMS AND CONTENT

Every day millions of people explain something to millions of other people. A policeman will tell a bewildered visitor how to find a tourist attraction; a doctor may tell a patient what diabetes is and how to cope with it; a parent will explain to a small child why it is dangerous to play too near the fire. In addition to these explanations outside the school system, there will be thousands of teachers working in classrooms who will explain a new concept, or a classroom rule, who will clarify confusion, maybe unlock a mystery. This book attempts to help new teachers learn how to master the art of clear explanation and to help experienced teachers to improve their skill at explaining.

Time invested in establishing or improving the ability to explain is time well spent. Sometimes, at the beginning of a lesson, a teacher will spend 5 or 10 minutes setting up what might be an hour's, a day's, a week's or even a term's work. Badly handled, this setting-up phase may be followed by mayhem as children, uncertain what they are supposed to do, or why they should do it, resort to asking one another, improvising or simply hoping the teacher will explain the task once more. Well conducted, however, a good explanation or introduction can motivate a class very effectively.

We once carried out a case study of a teacher who was shown in a research project to have secured the highest gains in learning of any teacher in the sample. Her explanations were a pleasure to witness. On one occasion she was telling a group of children about a maths worksheet on which they were about to embark. Many teachers would have simply handed the worksheets round and told pupils to get on with it, but she drew their attention to one or two of the questions, warned them that one particular question was tricky, reminded them of the principles on which the exercise was based, checked they all understood and concluded with, 'I can't wait to see what you make of number five'.

The speed and enthusiasm with which the group commenced was more reminiscent of the quest for the Holy Grail than completion of a maths worksheet.

The book is organized with the following six units.

In Unit 1 we discuss what an explanation actually is, what it consists of, its manifold purposes and the viewpoint of pupils.

Unit 2 investigates the various strategies employed by people when explaining, including the use of questions, the type of structure to be found in explanations and the use of ancillary aids.

Unit 3 explores levels of explanation, the analysis of explaining using observation schedules and other approaches, and also the need to match explanations to individuals and groups.

Unit 4 touches on important aspects of any explanation, that is, its actual content, the subject matter it covers, and the coping strategies that are developed, given that teachers cannot have in their grasp all the knowledge in the world.

Unit 5 describes strategies for explaining which appear to be effective if skilfully employed – the use of an appropriate language register; the place of analogies; the qualities of clarity and fluency; the ability to listen and use pupils' ideas.

Unit 6 concentrates on the evaluation of explanations, the kind of feedback that is available, the assessment of learning, and ways to improve one's own teaching in the light of experience.

How to use this book

It is possible for individuals or groups to work their way through this book, either with or without a tutor, but there is great benefit for either experienced or novice teachers to work collaboratively with others on some of the activities. There is nothing more beneficial to a school than a feeling that all are working together to improve their individual and collective professional competence.

The text can simply be read in its own right by anyone wanting to reflect on explanation or explaining, or work alone on teaching competence.

The discussion activities can be undertaken by trainees or experienced teachers, or for that matter by both groups working together, for it is of benefit to both beginners and seasoned practitioners to explore the fresh and the experienced view of professional competence.

The written activities can be done by individuals, but also by groups. They can also be discussed orally when they have been completed.

The practical activities are designed to be undertaken by teachers either in their own classroom or as experiments with small groups of children or with individuals. You should not hesitate to modify these to suit the age, background, interests and ability of the children concerned.

The written and discussion activities provide ideas for about 1 to $1\frac{1}{2}$ hours of work, the practical activities usually require a shorter amount of time in the actual classroom, but can easily take a similar 1 to $1\frac{1}{2}$ hours for follow-up.

The following symbols are used throughout the book to denote:

 quotations from published materials

 activities

transcripts of children or teachers talking during lessons

WHAT IS EXPLAINING?

Explaining something clearly to a pupil lies at the very centre of a good teacher's professional repertoire. It is not, however, a single type of activity, and the words 'explain' and 'explanation' can be used in different ways. Consider these four statements:

1 'Why are you two messing about when I've already told you once not to? I want an explanation.'

2 'Miss, can you explain how to do this sum?'

3 'You've just been told by the garage that you'll have to buy a new battery? That explains why your car wouldn't start.'

4 'Can you give me an explanation of why water freezes in winter?'

In the first statement, the quest for an 'explanation' is probably a prelude to a reprimand. The children are not really being asked for an account of personality factors, genetic endowment or environmental influences on their personal and social development. Just imagine the teacher's reaction if the child's 'explanation' began, 'According to experts on ethnology, rough-and-tumble play is a well-documented feature in the behaviour of young primates.' In this context the request for an 'explanation' is expected to produce a feeble justification or an apology.

In the second example, the response may be a brief clarification and reminder of a specific technique already learned, like how to multiply or divide two digit numbers, or it may involve a fundamental explanation of what a particular mathematical transaction involves, to a pupil who has no understanding whatsoever of it. The third example, on the other hand, is the identification of a simple relationship between cause and effect: the car would not start owing to a dying battery.

In the fourth case, the 'explanation' could vary enormously in complexity. A satisfactory answer

from a 6 year old might be that water freezes 'because it's very cold in winter'. An 11 year old might be expected to say, 'because the temperature has dropped below freezing point, which is 0 degrees centigrade'. A Nobel prizewinner might write a treatise on the structure of matter at differing temperatures, which could be incomprehensible to the lay audience.

We shall take as our operational definition, therefore, the statement:

'Explaining is giving understanding to another.'

This definition takes for granted that there are numerous contexts in which this may occur, many forms that explanations may take, and varying degrees of, and criteria for, success.

An explanation can help someone understand:

- *concepts* – including those which are new or familiar to the learner, like 'density' or 'prejudice';
- *cause and effect* – that rain is produced by the cooling of air, that a flat battery causes car-starting problems;
- *procedures* – classroom rules, homework requirements, how to convert a fraction to a decimal, how to ensure safety during gymnastics;
- *purposes and objectives* – why children are studying their local village, what they can expect to have learned at the conclusion of a particular task;
- *relationships* – between people, things or events: why footballers and pop-stars are both called (sometimes mistakenly) 'entertainers', why flies and bees are insects but spiders are not, what are the common features of religious festivals like Christmas and Easter;
- *processes* – how machines work, how animals or people behave.

There are numerous other kinds of explanation, and also there are variations of the categories given above. For example, explaining *consequences* can be similar, but is not necessarily identical to *cause and effect* explanation. The *consequence* of putting your hand into scalding water will be intense pain and a visit to the hospital. A *cause and effect* explanation might concentrate on how intense heat destroys tissue and what causes pain, but an explanation of *consequences* might look at such matters as the foolishness of an action, its effect on others as well as the victim, and the cost in time and money of treating self-imposed injury. Furthermore, some explanations can cover more than one category. Explaining to a class what the Roman wall is, could involve *concepts* ('aggression', 'defence'), *cause and effect* (what led to the wall being built), *processes* and *procedures* (how the wall was built, on whose authority) and *purposes* (to keep out the enemy).

 **ACTIVITY 1**

Let a member of the group:

1 Choose a hobby or interest he or she has. Just *one* key aspect of this should then be explained to the rest, taking no more than 4 or 5 minutes. There are countless possibilities, such as: what I like about chess; my favourite twentieth-century building; a simple recipe; getting rid of litter; how to lose weight; an effective advert; why lifeboats don't sink; the best (or worst) thing about being a parent, or having an older brother/sister; home insulation; the play/piece of music/poem/ painting that moved me most; and numerous others.

2 Analyse the nature of the explanation, using, if possible, a sound tape or video of it. What were the key concepts? What types of explanation were involved? How effective an explanation was it, and why?

3 Consider what differences and similarities there might have been if the explanation had been directed to:
   (i)   a 5 year old;
   (ii) a 9 year old;
   (iii) an intelligent Martian.

4 Let the person have a second attempt at explaining a different topic, or the same one, in the light of feedback.

Main features

Activity 1 should demonstrate a number of fundamental features of effective explaining. First of all there are several *keys* which help to unlock understanding. A key may be a central principle or a generalization. It may contain an example or an analogy. For instance, if someone is describing a recipe for making an omelette then the notion of *heat* would be central. If too little heat is applied eggs will not set, if too much is used then the eggs will burn.

It is not too difficult to see other keys to understanding how to cook an omelette. The question of *taste* will occur, and thus the addition of flavourings like salt and pepper, or fillings like cheese or mushroom. *Texture* is also important, hence the need to beat the eggs so that yolk and white mix evenly and to introduce air so the omelette will be light. The great chef Escoffier used to put little pieces of butter into the egg mixture which melted during cooking and affected both taste and texture, so this might be a concrete example used to illustrate one or more of the central notions or keys in the explanation. Where omelettes are concerned, the difference between a good and a bad explanation could be the difference between an Escoffier masterpiece and a poultice. Introduce a key concept like *health* and the need to avoid too much salt and too many dairy products, and to cook eggs to a certain temperature to prevent salmonella, and you may not have your omelette at all!

There is more to an explanation, however, than a bunch of keys. The *voice* of the explainer is important. The same text given to someone with a pleasant, well-modulated voice and another person with a flat, tedious delivery, will sound quite different. Correct use of voice involves light and shade, knowing when to slow down or accelerate, which words or phrases to emphasize, when to pause, how to read the audience so that the appropriate tone of voice is used, hushed for something serious, light for something frivolous or humorous. Sometimes voice is amplified by gesture, pointing to something, spreading arms to indicate size or breadth, difficult for those who feel inhibited, but, well used, an amplification of the voice. Imagine you are doing a radio broadcast about teaching science in the primary school. Try saying the following sentence in different tones of voice:

'Science can be very exciting for children, because they'll learn about some of the most spectacular phenomena in the universe; but, if they're badly taught, science will seem a tedious chore.'

Voice and gesture can amplify explanations

If you speak the words in a flat monotone, it will sound as dreary as the condemnation of bad teaching suggests. For effective communication you may choose to emphasize words like 'exciting', 'spectacular' or 'badly'. You may pause after 'but' and slow down on the words 'tedious chore'. Your voice may rise in pitch during the 'exciting' first half of the statement, and fall at the dreary foreboding of the second part.

There are several aspects of *structure* that are important. If an explanation has several keys in it, maybe three or four principal features that need to be brought out, then thought must be given to such matters as the *sequence* of ideas, how you should begin, which notion should be unwrapped or explored first, which second, which left till last, how you might conclude. These matters cannot always be fully determined in advance, of course, as once children are engaged by an explanation, their questions, insights, confusion or suggestions will begin to take over and affect the process.

Questions about *structure* are closely related to those about *teaching strategies*. What use should be made of questions? (See the companion book in this series on *Questioning* by the same authors.) What is the place of a demonstration? Of practical work by the children? Of individual, group or whole-class teaching? How much and what sort of practice may be needed if the children are learning a concept, like what a fraction is, or a skill, like how to shape a piece of wood with a file? What sort of aids to teaching might help – a picture; a video; a model; a piece of equipment?

In turn, thoughts about *teaching strategies* are partly contingent on the *purpose* of the explanation. Is it to teach a fact; a skill; a concept; a form of attitude or behaviour? In health education, for example, if children are learning about dental care, then one principal objective would be to ensure that they clean their teeth and avoid tooth decay. The teacher may have to explain *facts* (what causes tooth decay, what prevents it, like regular brushing, avoiding certain foods, using fluoride toothpaste and anti-plaque mouthwash); *skills* such as how to clean your teeth properly (trendy dentists nowadays recommend circular movements of the brush, rather than just side to side, or up and down); *attitudes*, like why it is worth cleaning your teeth properly (it is preferable to pain); and *behaviour* (ensuring that children really do clean their teeth, rather than just appear sanctimonious about it). The payoff for successful explaining of the first three – facts, skills and attitudes – would be the last, that is, ensuring behaviour which avoided needless decay and discomfort, so the purpose of explanations in health education is

often clear, even if results are difficult to achieve.

Within a certain overall purpose there may be a set of shorter-term objectives. For example, in order to give an explanation of how to avoid dental decay, the teacher may decide to make the opening gambit one which will arouse interest or intrigue the class, saying, 'In a minute I'm going to tell you why my uncle can't eat raspberries and walnuts any more, even though he loves them, but first I want to know if anyone's ever had toothache.' This device is known as a '*tease*' in broadcasting, and many radio and television programmes begin with a tease: 'And in a packed programme today we'll be meeting the man who can play the oboe underwater, and we'll be telling you how you can save thousands of pounds without effort, but first the news headlines.' It is one of many ways of both gaining attention and shaping the presentation of information.

ACTIVITY 2

1 Imagine you are starting a project on 'Energy' with a class of children aged about 9, which might run for 4 or 5 weeks. Decide how you might explain what 'Energy' actually is, asking yourself:
 (i) What are the key concepts children will need to understand?
 (ii) How could I find out what children already know?
 (iii) How would I introduce the topic?
 (iv) What sort of strategies, activities, materials would I need?

2 Compare your ideas with those of others in your group. What is in common and what is different? Have you identified similar key concepts/strategies?

3 Try out your idea with a group of children, if you have the opportunity; you can modify it, as appropriate, if you can only have them for a short period of time. Look at the following:
 (i) Did the children already know more or less about 'Energy' than you thought?
 (ii) How effectively did they learn the key concepts?
 (iii) Would they, for example, be able to write or talk about human energy? fuels? how energy is used in toys?
 (iv) If you have been able to make a sound tape or video tape of your session, are there any interesting events worthy of further thought – a good question you or a child asked, someone being puzzled, a good illustrative example you used?

(v)　How would you explain the topic next time in the light of your experience?

The pupil's perspective

There are usually at least two parties in an explanation, the explainer and what you might call the 'explainee', the person to whom something is being explained. Adult life is full of such pairs, and sometimes, as in classroom teaching, explanations can be reciprocal: person A explains to person B, and then, in turn, person B explains to person A. A doctor may begin a consultation by asking the patient to explain the pain or the symptoms causing concern. At this point the patient is the explainer. Once the doctor has made a diagnosis, roles are reversed and the doctor now explains the nature of the ailment to the patient. A similar process occurs when we call in someone to mend our car or television set and, in the classroom, when children explain to their teacher what it is they do not understand.

We once ran a microteaching session with a group of teacher trainees. The students each took about ten children and had to introduce a topic like 'Sea Travel' or 'Volcanoes' in any way they chose. They were then videotaped and, following analysis of the video, were able to have a second chance with a different group of ten children from the same class of 9 and 10 year olds. In her first attempt Helen, a conscientious student, launched her carefully prepared model of a volcano with a torrent of information: 'Today I want to tell you a little bit about volcanoes. Here is a model of one and you can see that this is the crater and, as you probably know, this is the lava, and this part here is called the magma chamber. Perhaps you've heard of volcanoes before. There's one in Italy called Vesuvius . . .'

Seeing the lack of opportunity for the children to respond to her 'as you probably know' and 'perhaps you've heard of' statements, in her second attempt she showed the children her model and asked if anyone knew anything about volcanoes. To her surprise a collection of information began to emerge from this new group of children, things seen on television, or learned from books, friends or relatives, that went way beyond what she had told the first group of children. Some mention was made of Vesuvius, Etna, Krakatoa and the volcanic dust that travelled round the world, Surtsey, craters on the moon, Icelandic geysers and Tristan da Cunha, and terms like 'lava' and 'eruption' emerged

naturally. This approach gave her a much clearer idea of the level at which to pitch the explanation of volcanoes and volcanic activity, as well as an indication of which children had a sophisticated understanding of the topic and which needed a basic grounding.

One reason for trying to elicit from the pupils what they already know is to help with choice of a suitable *language register*. Doctors have to make decisions everyday about what words and phrases to use with patients who have different backgrounds. Some may cope easily with medical terms, others may need analogies (It's like a car running out of petrol) or more familiar everyday language (waterworks). With adult learners or older secondary school pupils, a teacher might use a phrase like 'inversely proportional' in a maths or physics lesson. For primary pupils, many not yet able to grasp abstract concepts, the teacher might say, 'The more you have of this, the less you have of that', or with younger children, 'It's like a seesaw, the higher this side is, the lower that one is.'

Another strong reason for establishing what pupils already understand about a new topic or concept prior to a course of explanation is to clarify any misconceptions which might occur. Suppose, for example, you were teaching about floating and sinking. If you simply gave children experiments, or delivered a short lecturette on the topic, you might not realize that children had acquired incorrect assumptions which needed to be unlearned. Even a simple opening question like, 'Which things float in water and which things sink?' might reveal that some children wrongly believe that heavy objects invariably sink and light objects always float. Yet a 1,000-ton ship floats and a tiny pebble sinks. Knowing about misconceptions provides valuable information prior to an explanation. As the cartoon on p. 8 shows, failure to appreciate the impact of an explanation because the explainer is unaware of the complexity of it to the recipient, or uses the wrong language, or does not appreciate what the learner understands or misunderstands, can be a disaster. The explainer can be very pleased with, from his vantage point, an explanation clearly delivered, yet the poor beggar who is supposed to be enlightened can be left feeling utterly confused.

Most important of all, from the pupil's point of view, explaining has often been shown to be the skill most appreciated by pupils. A study of several thousand pupils in Birmingham in the 1930s showed that, of a list of seven teaching skills, the ability to explain clearly was placed first. Fifty years later we conducted another survey of 200

pupils, this time using a list of 32 teaching skills, and again the ability to explain was in first place (Wragg 1984).

Summary

Explaining is the giving of understanding to another. It can involve children learning about:
- concepts;
- cause and effect;
- procedures;
- purposes and objectives;
- relationships;
- processes;
- consequences;
- a host of other notions.

Unlocking understanding may be done in numerous ways. These include:

- the identification of keys (central concepts, principles);

- effective use of voice and gesture;
- clearly structured explanations;
- proper sequencing of ideas and linking of keys;
- deployment of a range of teaching strategies to teach knowledge, skills attitudes and behaviour;
- using appropriate teaching aids.

The pupil's perspective is especially important. To avoid confusion try to:

- find out what individual children already know and understand about the topic or concept;
- use an appropriate language register with sensible choice of words and phrases appropriate to the context;
- find out about misconceptions which need to be unlearned.

Other units in this book will cover some of these matters in greater detail. To conclude this section, try the following activity either alone or with others. It brings together some of the points covered in this unit.

 ACTIVITY 3

1 Look out for examples of the following in your own teaching or in that of another teacher or student you are observing. Make brief notes after your lesson (or during the lesson if you are observing someone else) in the spaces below.

(i)   An explanation of a concept:

(ii)   An explanation of a procedure:

(iii) A key point in an explanation:

(iv) An example of a child's misconception or erroneous view of something:

(v)   A particular word or phrase which needed to be clarified for a pupil:

2 Consider how effectively each of these was handled, what the teacher did and what the pupil(s) did.

3 If you are in a group, discuss your notes with others who have done the same sort of analysis.

STRATEGIES OF EXPLANATION

Many explanations are given in answer to questions, sometimes actual questions which children have asked, like:

'What colour paints do I have to mix to get purple?'

Sometimes they are hypothetical questions, as, for example, when a teacher explains what the children will do on a field trip she has arranged, even though no one may yet have enquired about the detail. Indeed the common interrogatives Who? What? How? Why? Where? When? – offer clues to the nature of different types of explanation.

'Who?' questions often produce explanations of relationships. An account of the Romans in Britain might explain who they were and the fact that their relationship with Britons was as conquerors. 'How?' questions, on the other hand, may lead to an evaluation of a process. Exploration of how people in a neighbourhood earn their living could involve learning about farming, factory work or transportation. 'Why?' questions lead to an understanding of purposes and objectives. If a teacher were asked to explain why babies cry, this could involve such reasons as 'to signal pain', 'to obtain food', 'to express frustration' and so on. However, most of these explanations in answer to interrogatives are not of a single kind. A 'Why?' question might equally provoke an explanation of a process, not just a purpose. Many scientific 'Why?' questions, like 'Why does a magnet pick up iron?' or 'Why do things fall down and not up?' elicit an explanation that covers both a process and a concept, such as 'gravity'. Wrapped inside a 'Why?' question is often a 'How?' question.

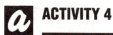

ACTIVITY 4

1 A class of 8 to 9 year olds is discussing ideas for topics about which they might write in their class newspaper. One possibility is the 'Neighbourhood Watch' scheme. Read this transcript from the lesson, as the scheme is explained.

※ _____

Teacher:	What else can we write about? Has anybody heard of the 'Neighbourhood Watch' scheme? What is it?
Pupil 1:	You put a sticker in your window.
Teacher:	Yes, that's right, but what is the scheme exactly, does anyone know? . . . (no response) . . . Well, it's to stop burglars. The idea is that everybody in the same street will keep an eye open for burglars or anything suspicious, and then they ring the police up if they see somebody trying to get into a house to steal something. So you know what the 'Neighbourhood Watch' scheme is now?
Pupil 2:	My nanny and grandad are in one.
Teacher:	What is the 'Neighbourhood Watch' scheme, Richard? Can you tell me?
Pupil 2:	It's to stop burglars stealing things.
Pupil 3:	What happens if you come home and find they've stolen your video?
Teacher:	Well, if you come home and find that that's not there, you know you've had a thief in the house, don't you?
Pupil 4:	What if you think you've been burgled and it's only a magpie?
Teacher:	Well, I don't know, that's a tricky one. Well, if you see something suspicious you report it. You might think it's a magpie, but it could have been a real burglar. Magpies don't very often steal things like that, do they? Unless you've got an open window and a very shiny diamond ring on the sill.

2 Look at the *strategies* employed by both the teacher and the pupils to develop understanding of the 'Neighbourhood Watch' scheme. What is clear and what is vague?

Different approaches

During the Leverhulme Primary Project we often asked several teachers to explain the same topic or concept to their class. It was most interesting to see the range of explanations and the variety of strategies employed. One of the topics was 'Insects' and here are just some of the strategies employed by different teachers observed during the research project.

A factual exposition: A straightforward explanation by the teacher describing body shape, number of legs, wings, etc.

A closed question: To which there is a single, verifiable textbook answer, e.g. 'How many legs do insects have?' or 'Is a spider an insect?'

An open question: To which there are several answers, e.g. 'Who can tell me something about insects?'

A focused question: For example, 'What sort of things does an insect have on its head?' These questions may be partly open, in that there are several possible answers, yet partly closed, in the sense that the answers are verifiable as correct or incorrect, but focused specifically on one particular aspect of the explanation.

Probing questions: Sometimes teachers use a sequence of probing questions, persisting with the same line of questioning, but seeking greater depth and clarity, as, for example, in the following:

Teacher: What are these for?
Pupil: They're feelers.
Teacher: Yes, but what are they for?

Explaining about insects

Pupil: Feeling things.
Teacher: Yes, but what exactly do they do? What does the insect use them for?

Another example:

Teacher: Would you like to tell me what an insect is, Daniel?
Pupil: An animal with six legs.
Teacher: Six legs, so if I took a centipede and pulled off 94 legs, would that make it an insect?

Teaching specialist terms:

Teacher: Do you know what that part of the body is called?
Pupil: The middle bit.
Teacher: No, it's got a posh word – the thorax.

Humour:

Pupil: He's got antlers though.
Teacher: (smiles) *What* did you say, Simon? (children laugh) He's nearly right though. What are they really called?

Teacher makes a joke about Simon confusing 'antlers' and 'antennae'.

Praise: Frequent use was observed of teachers praising correct answers or comments, either with a simple 'good' or more effusively.
Chiding: A few observations of reprimands for incorrect answers, usually when the pupil had not taken the issue seriously. Incorrect answers were more frequently corrected by the teacher or else another pupil was called on to correct the error.
Practical work: Children handled real insects, or looked at models or specimens in perspex cases. Some made insect shapes out of coloured pipe cleaners.
Pictures: Teachers gave out photographs or drawings of insects.
Analogy/example: Often teachers will give or elicit an example, 'A house-fly is an insect', or use an analogy:

Teacher: Now insects' eyes are rather special, not like ours. The insect's eye is made up of hundreds of separate tiny eyes, very sensitive to movement. Its eye looks almost like a plastic bag of marbles; the plastic bag is the whole eye and the marbles are the mini eyes or lenses.

Use of the 'plastic bag of marbles' as a concrete analogy.

'Not' analogy/example: Just as a teacher might say something is 'like' something else, so too teachers used 'not' analogies and examples as a means of contrast. Among instances were:

'Is a bird an insect?'

'What's the difference between an elephant and an insect?'

'Is a cow an insect?'

Involving imagination: Even in a factual explanation, some teachers involved pupils' imagination. Examples were:

'What do you think it must feel like to be an insect?'

'Do you know that butterflies can taste with their feet? (pupils laugh). Yes, when they land on things they can taste them using their feet. Wouldn't it be funny if we could taste with our feet!'

A 'tease': Some teachers began their explanation with a 'tease'.

Teacher: If I told you in, say, a bucket of earth there were hundreds of them. They're in the air, they're even in ponds and rivers. There are millions of them in a tree. They live all over the world, except at the North and South Poles. There are over a million different types of them. There are 200,000 different types in this country alone. Some of them can fly, some can swim, some make holes in the ground and some make holes in wood. What do you think I would be talking about?

A 'tease' need not be a superficial attention-getting gimmick. The notable feature of this 'tease' is the richness of information in it.

Practical work: making a model of an insect

Anecdote/story: Several teachers used a personal anecdote about a bee or a butterfly, or invited children to tell these. Some use a short story:

✳ _____

Teacher: Shall I tell you a story? Many years ago, when I was a little boy, in China the Chinese people decided to kill thousands of millions of birds because they were eating all the crops. The next Spring, guess what happened. All the caterpillars ate the crops, because there were no birds to kill the caterpillars!

Summary

At the end of the session it was common, though not inevitable, to find some kind of summary, sometimes by the pupils, sometimes by the teachers, sometimes by both:

✳ _____

Teacher: So then, let's go back to my little friend here (teacher points to model of an insect). Who's going to tell me the names of the parts?
Pupil: Head.
Teacher: Head, yes.
Pupil: Thorax and abdomen.
Teacher: Well done. What are these?
Pupil: Feelers.
Teacher: And what are they for?
Pupil: Tasting the air.
Teacher: Yes, 'tasting' the air, that's a good description.

These many different strategies and tactics show something of the infinite range of possibilities when explaining to children. Explaining is not a single entity, not a unidimensional monochrome skill, but rather a repertoire of skills requiring much of what teachers need in daily professional life – planning, management and organization, the ability to ask intelligent, varied and appropriate questions, clarity, involvement of pupils, practical work, the use of teaching aids and numerous other aspects of competency. There are many times when children are busily engaged in activities from which they are learning and they are, therefore, in a sense explaining things to themselves; but frequently, when teachers and pupils are interacting together, teaching *is* explaining. It is the single predominant purpose, so it needs to be done well.

The broad strategies

In later units we shall be dealing specifically with some of the particular strategies mentioned above, but at this point it is important to reflect on some of the broad categories like preparation, openings, questioning, practical work and the use of teaching aids, the structure of explanations and summary.

Preparation and planning

A great deal of what happens in teaching is spontaneous and unrehearsed, unanticipated even. When teachers begin to explain a new topic or a classroom procedure to young children, before long the children's responses, their questions, insights, looks of puzzlement, smiles or frowns, will, if the teacher is sensitive to them, begin to affect the nature and direction of the explanation. Consider the messages, amplifications, opportunities and distractions in this exchange with 6 and 7 year olds:

Teacher:	We're going to make a little tortoise out of card today. Now, can anybody tell me something about a tortoise?
Pupil 1:	It's got a shell.
Teacher:	That's right, Nicola, it's got a nice shell.
Pupil 2:	I'm going to make a turtle, a green one.
Teacher:	Well turtles are like tortoises, aren't they? How do tortoises move?
Pupil 3:	Slow. Plod, plod, plod, plod.
Pupil 4:	My brother had a tortoise, but it died.
Pupil 5:	You've got to feed it proper food, or it dies.

With younger children especially, their own thoughts and concerns are close to the surface and they are eager to express them. In the above exchanges the teacher was intending to focus in particular on the shape and movement of tortoises, as the children were going to assemble a simple 'motor' out of a bobbin, a matchstick and an elastic band, and then cover it with a piece of folded circular card, complete with head and tail, to make a slow-moving tortoise. In order to maintain the interest of the pupils and secure their commitment to the activity, the teacher was prepared to listen to anecdotes about turtles and tortoises that died, but ultimately the children had to be shown how to make the tortoise, even though there was plenty of scope for variety and for children's own ideas.

The tortoise-making lesson is an interesting example of what preparation is needed for a successful explanation of the activity. Clearly, in order for several children to make such tortoises, the teacher will need to provide sufficient materials, so some of the planning will be related to resourcing the activity properly, but we are concentrating here on the forethought that will be necessary for the actual setting-up phase of the lesson. We take these under three headings: first-, second- and third-order considerations.

First order   The *general purpose* of the activity, for example: to teach children how to design and make something; that children should learn about energy in a simple machine (the elastic band in the bobbin).
Second order   What the *keys* are in the explanation? What central concepts, skills or processes need to be explained, e.g. how things can be made to move (the place of 'energy'); how to fit the elastic band through the bobbin; how to secure it around the matchsticks at either end; how to cut out the tortoise shape from the card; how to paint or colour it to make it look attractive and also to make sure the pattern joins up over the seam; how to glue it together so it fits over the bobbin properly?
Third order   What *strategies* can effectively achieve these aims: what is best done with the whole group, what with a small group, what with individuals; what sort of questions might be asked; any demonstrations (for example, whether having a finished model to show how the whole thing works might be a help); how to secure the commitment and interest/involvement of the children (how they can use their imagination in the design and not merely feel they are doing a mechanical copying of someone else's idea, whether an initial 'tease' might work).

The fact that teachers need to give thought to the

preparation of explanations does not rule out children playing a significant part in them. Indeed, skilful teachers ensure that children's ideas and suggestions play a central role from the beginning, even though these will make the pattern of development to some extent unpredictable. Nevertheless, having initial thoughts about purpose, key notions and a deft strategy or two is a wise investment of planning time for the explaining, setting-up phase of the activity.

Openings

The opening to an explanation cannot be seen as entirely separate from the whole thing. There is no point in staging some spectacular opening move, only to find that children remember nothing more than the gimmick. Ultimately, something important must be learned and all the opening can do is set the scene and prepare the way for what follows.

There was an old tip given to university academics before they delivered their first lecture. It ran: 'Tell them what you're going to tell them. Tell them. Tell them what you've told them.' It was a crude tip and, judging by the lectures some of us have had to endure, often ignored, but the general shape of opening/exposition/recapitulation, offered some degree of structure for what was potentially a rambling, shapeless hour of presentation.

The 'Tell them what you're going to tell them' sort of opening, is sometimes referred to as an *advance organizer*. It can be especially useful when teaching individual or sets of concepts, particularly if these are complex. There is debate in educational research about how effective advance organizers are (Ausubel *et al.* 1978), for though there is some evidence to suggest children given advance organizers achieve better understanding and higher test scores, this sort of research has not always been well conducted, and is in any case notoriously difficult to carry out, given that advance organizers are but one of several devices that teachers use. It is also open to argument whether telling people what they will do spoils the mystery, or even actually reduces motivation.

Consider, however, the use made by the German playwright Bertolt Brecht of a narrator at the beginning of each scene in his play *Life of Galileo*. This narrator, in a few lines and often with the aid of a caption, tells the audience what is going to occur:

On the 22nd of June, 1633, before the Inquisition, Galileo Galilei recants his teaching about the movement of the Earth.

June twenty-second, sixteen thirty-three
A momentous date for you and me.
Of all the days that was the one
An age of reason could have begun.

Does it ruin the play now that we know Galileo will recant in the coming scene, for fear of being tortured by the Inquisition? Probably no more than knowing at the beginning of Shakespeare's *Julius Caesar* that Brutus and Cassius will kill Caesar, or being told by the three witches in *Macbeth* what is going to happen next.

Openings or explanations can have several purposes, therefore:

- to organize in advance what is to come;
- to intrigue and arouse curiosity;
- to discover what children already know about the topic;
- to refresh children's memories of what has been learned or done previously, prior to explaining the new material or process.

Openings may contain any or all of these ingredients, and teachers need to give careful thought to the topic before deciding which kind of opening to use.

@ ACTIVITY 5

1 Imagine you are teaching the topic 'Insects' to a class of primary children who are learning about them for the first time. Plan three different openings which cover each of the following:

   (i)   arousing curiosity
   (ii) finding out what children already know about insects
   (iii) using an advance organizer to signal what the children are going to learn about insects

2 Look carefully at the three sets of strategies you have chosen. Which would you prefer? Is it possible and/or desirable to combine two or more of your ideas in the same opening?

3 If you have the opportunity, compare your ideas with those of others in your group.

Questioning

Questions asked by teachers and pupils are an integral part of many explanations. The companion volume *Questioning*, written by the same two authors as this present book, deals with the matter in much greater detail, so we shall not devote as much space to it here as the topic would justify.

Within explanations, questioning can serve several purposes. These include:

- to find out what pupils already know, or do not know;
- to shape the line of argument by using pupil's own ideas;
- to check how well pupils understand what is being explained;
- to elicit concrete examples of principles or concepts;
- to help children develop a desire to enquire and learn further, once the explanation is complete.

Different kinds of question can fulfil these various purposes. For example, both closed and open questions can be used to find out what children already know. Suppose a class is studying magnetism, a teacher might ask a closed question, like, 'Does a magnet pick up plastic?' or a more open question such as, 'Can anyone tell me what magnets do and do not pick up?'

The questions can stand alone or be related to practical work. The teacher might say: 'I've given you twelve different things, like a piece of rubber, a paper clip, a plastic tube, a brass rod, a 2-inch nail, and so on. Now I want you to answer two questions. The first is: "Which of these things will the magnet pick up?" Make a guess and then put things you think a magnet will pick up into your "Yes" pile. The second question is: "Which of these things will the magnet *not* pick up?" Put those into your "No" pile. Then I'll give you a magnet and you can see if you're right or not.' The response to these questions would show whether the children already knew some basic principles of magnetism; whether they were completely ignorant and merely assigned the objects randomly; or whether they had a partial understanding, but certain misconceptions, like believing erroneously that magnets attracted all metals, instead of just those with iron in them.

Similarly, questions can be used in sequence, either to probe more deeply into an issue, or to take understanding on to higher levels. We return to this topic in Unit 3. Eliciting examples is also a common purpose for questioning ('Can anyone give me an example of an insect?', 'Who can tell me the name of a shape with right angles in it?').

One of the most challenging kinds of question is the one, often towards the end of an explanatory phase, which poses questions that can only be answered by further study. This is an effective means of motivating pupils to learn after the initial explanation is complete. One teacher we observed con-

cluded her opening phase on 'Diet and Health' by saying, 'So these are some of the things we need to eat to keep ourselves healthy. But we've also talked about food which doesn't do us much good, and might even do us some harm. What I want you to ask yourself is this, "Is the food I eat good for me, or bad for me?" That's why we're all, me included, going to keep a diary of every single thing we eat, and then we'll analyse just how healthy our diet really is.' This personalized question proved a strong motivator as the children went on to study their own food intake over several days.

Practical work and the use of teaching aids

There are numerous theories about how children learn, some complementary, some contradictory. Amongst the best-known and most cited views of primary age children are those of Piaget and Bruner. Piaget's stages of development posit that most infant school children will be at the 'intuitive' stage, able to form vague impressions, but not always to put these into words, and that in junior schools most will be in the 'concrete operational' stage, capable of logical thinking with concrete things, but not yet able to operate in the abstract. Bruner used the terms 'enactive' for the first stage of development when children see objects in terms of what they *do* to or with them, like touch, hold or throw them, and subsequently the 'iconic' stage, when single features, like colour, shape or sound, may dominate children's view of the world. The 'symbolic' stage, when children cope with logic and various symbol systems, comes last.

There has been considerable controversy over the theories of both Piaget and Bruner, but their writings have drawn attention, as have many other writers, including their critics, to the importance for young children of personal practical experience. Abstract concepts can indeed be learned and reproduced mechanically by primary children, but relatively few will understand these if they are simply learned as slogans rather than understood as concepts. A combination of practical work and sound learning of relevant, factual information, however, can lead to understanding of quite complex ideas even by young children. Theatre companies like the Molecule Theatre, for example, have shown that children can learn, through drama and personal experience, important concepts in the physical sciences.

Similarly, the use by the teacher and/or the pupils of pictures, models, videos, games and posters can enhance learning for those not always able to grasp verbal explanations. When we studied classes of children learning about floating and sinking, it was

The magic of magnetism

clear that it was not an easy topic to study, and teachers themselves were not always clear about such matters as density, Archimedes' Principle or surface tension. However, those who had seen a video showing how lifeboats are built not to sink had a powerful visual memory of some of the principles shown graphically on film.

Practical activities and visual aids, therefore, need to be designed or selected so that:
- they are appropriate to the age and background of the pupils;
- they enhance and amplify the concepts, principles or processes being explained;
- they are integral to the explanation, not mere adjuncts to it or gimmicks;
- they are not confusing and do not confound or cloud the explanation.

The structure of explanations

To some extent the structure of an explanation should help determine its strategies. It is equally arguable, however, that the strategies determine the structure. This paradox depends on teachers' preferred teaching styles and the subject matter. In subjects like mathematics, it is sometimes the case that A must precede B, that unless you can calculate the square of a number and also multiply two numbers, you cannot calculate the area of a circle since this involves both operations. In explanations, therefore, where there is a logical *linear* sequence, it is important to take first things first, that is, to work out the first principles, explain these, and then move on to the next stage.

Not all subject matter falls into this kind of logical sequencing. In history, for example, it might sometimes be essential to sequence the explanation of events in chronological order, but there is also an argument for a different order on occasions. For

Mathematics – logical and linear?

example, if children already know about the Spanish Armada, it might make sense to start off with a review of what they already know, or do not know, about the events of 1588, and then move back in time to explain what led up to the invasion.

Teachers' personal preferences also enter into the equation. Those who prefer an *a priori rational planning approach* may well want to determine structure in advance. Others who prefer an *intuitive empirical approach* may opt for 'suck-it-and-see', preferring to improvise more in the light of actual pupil response.

When explanations are analysed systematically, a number of features are often detected, and these will be discussed more fully in Unit 3. In addition to the *advance organizer* mentioned above, there are often *links* between the central *keys*. Links can often be identified by the prepositions and conjunctions that forge them, words like: because, since, as, in order to, as a result, and so, therefore, by, if ... then, the more ... the more. Examples of such links are:

'People first developed weapons *in order to* defend themselves and also hunt animals for food.'

'*If* you increase the size *then* you also increase the weight.'

'*The more* water you put into that paint *the more* messy it is.'

'You can stay in at playtime, *since* you can't behave yourself.'

'You can change the note on the recorder *by* putting your finger over the hole.'

Sometimes the structure of a certain part of an explanation may benefit from a mixture of approaches, provided they are coherent and not random. One frequently used mini-structure of this kind is to combine rules (or principles) and examples, often in the order:

rule – example(s) – rule

as in this instance:

Usually when we're spelling we put 'i' before 'e', except after the letter 'c'. So it's 'ie' in a word like thief, but 'ei' in 'receive'. Mostly you'll find it's 'ie', but look out for that letter 'c'.

Summary

When reaching closure, teachers employ numerous ways to see that children know what has been explained. The summary may be entirely by the *teacher*:

Teacher: Now let's see what we've learned. We've found out that magnets only pick up things with iron in them. Some people thought they picked up all metals, but they didn't attract brass, aluminium, copper or lead when we tried them out. And they only picked up the tin can lid because it's got some iron in it.

It may, alternatively, be by the *pupils*:

Teacher: Who can tell us what we've learned about insects?
Pupil 1: They've got six legs.
Pupil 2: And feelers and an abdomen.
Pupil 3: And a thorax and wings, and a spider's not an insect because it's got eight legs.
Pupil 4: The feelers are called 'antennae'.

It can also be by the *teachers and the pupils jointly*, with the teacher 'shaping' the summary:

Teacher: So what does the story tell us about the old man?
Pupil 1: That he's tired.
Teacher: Yes, that's right, but there was more to it than that.
Pupil 2: He's lived a busy life and he's not afraid of dying.
Teacher: And why wasn't he afraid of dying?
Pupil 3: Because he's religious and he believes there's life after death.

ACTIVITY 6

Choose a poem to read to the class and plan out a complete explanation of the principal feelings and messages it portrays. Think about:

1 How you would introduce it.

2 What words or phrases might need explaining.

3 What feelings or emotions might need exploring and/or explaining.

4 Who would read the poem.

5 What, if any, activities might be part of it, and what the sequence might be.

6 How the session on the poem might conclude.

ANALYSING EXPLANATIONS

Explanations occur by the dozen every day in primary teaching. Many teachers engage in a thousand or more exchanges with pupils every single day of their teaching career, giving information, asking a question, praising or reprimanding, listening to someone, settling a dispute, hearing a child read, talking socially with an individual or group. Events that happen with great frequency are well worth analysing in a deliberate and systematic way, for teachers can often slip into set ways of interacting with children. After countless repeats and rehearsals, favoured strategies then become like an old pair of gloves or slippers, so warm and well fitting, one is reluctant to change or discard them, even if they are worn out.

There are numerous ways of analysing explanations, just as there are several approaches to the analysis of classroom events. It is possible to use both *quantitative* methods, whereby certain aspects of teaching are looked for and tallied when they occur, and *qualitative* forms of analysis, which involve the study of particular events and episodes, the search for meaning, impact or effect and the roles played by participants. These approaches are different and can be complementary. It is not a question of whether one methodology is intrinsically better than another, but rather of what is the best approach in the circumstances. Questions like 'How often?' or 'How much?' may well be answered by an event-counting, quantifying approach. A question like 'What did the pupil understand by . . .?' may require an incisive case-study approach, since each child is an individual who may or may not react to situations in the same way as others in the same class.

Sometimes we want to know information in quantities – how many children got a sum right and how many got it wrong, for example, so that we know who may need extra help and who is ready to go on to more demanding work. On other occasions it is the unique nature of a problem or situation which is of more concern – why Catherine finds it difficult to understand subtraction, even if you have tried several different ways of explaining and have given her plenty of practice.

Quantitative analysis

In order to see some of the many different ways of analysing explanations, consider this episode in a class of 8 and 9 year olds. The teacher is explaining about the fictitious 'Island of Zarg', a map of which is before each child, prior to them writing an essay about it.

Teacher:	Can you see anything that attracts you about the island? Anywhere you'd like to visit, David?
Pupil 1:	Castle Point.
Teacher:	Why would you like to go there?
Pupil 1:	It's exciting.
Teacher:	Yes, it's exciting. Have you found anywhere you'd like to go, Emma?
Pupil 2:	I think . . .
Teacher:	No, it's Emma's turn. I'd like to hear what Emma has to say.
Pupil 3:	Eastern Moors. There's a creature . . . it's . . . it's . . .
Teacher:	There's something up there that Emma's found. What has she found coming out of the sea?
Pupil 4:	A monster.
Teacher:	Yes, it could be. What's coming out of his hand?
Pupil 2:	Lightning.
Teacher:	What else has he got coming out of him?
Pupil 2:	Rain.

Teacher: Rain and thunder, so it's almost as if he's in control of the ...?

Pupil 2: Weather.

Teacher: The weather, yes, I think so ... What would be a good word to describe Darkling Forest?

Pupil 3: Spooky and creepy.

Teacher: Better than spooky and creepy?

Pupil 3: Strange and weird.

Teacher: Yes, strange and weird. How about a word beginning with two e's? Do you know it?

Pupil 1: Eerie.

Teacher: Yes. What does eerie mean?

Pupil 1: Scary.

There are many *quantitative* conclusions one could reach about this short episode, some interesting, some banal. By way of example a few are listed on p. 22. Not all quantitative analysis is clear-cut, however, even if it looks precise.

Quantitative information like that given on p. 22, standing alone, tells us little about the quality of the teaching, about what the pupils have learned, about such important matters as the clarity of the explanation, or, if factual material is involved, the accuracy and correctness of what is being taught. Taken into consideration alongside additional information, however, it can be quite interesting and valuable, especially when related to other significant information, like the purposes and intentions of the lesson. For example, suppose the teacher wants to involve several children in the discussion. To get four of them to contribute in about one minute might seem to be not too bad. On the other hand, suppose the teacher really wanted to develop the children's ability not only to write

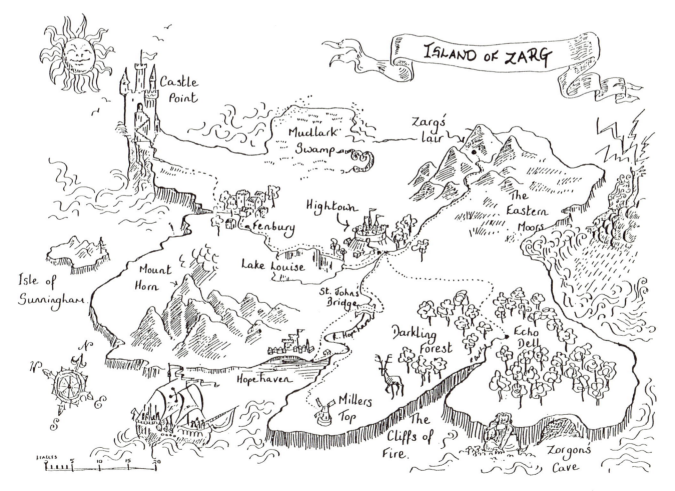

Island of Zarg

Quantitative analysis of Island of Zarg

Pupils participating	4	
Teacher's questions	12	
Open questions	7	(approx.)
Closed questions	5	(approx.)
Statements of approval	5	
Statements of disapproval	2	
Reprimands	1	
Length of episode	68	seconds
Total number of words uttered	164	
Words spoken by teacher	138	
Words spoken by pupils	26	
Percentage teacher talk	84	%
Percentage pupil talk	16	%
Length of pauses	19	seconds
Length of talk	49	seconds
Number of teacher utterances	12	
Number of pupil utterances	12	
Percentage of talk	72	%
Percentage of non-talk (pauses, etc.)	28	%
Average length of each teacher utterance	11.5	words
Average length of each pupil utterance	2.17	words
Number of keys (i) Where to visit		
(ii) Why place attracts		
(iii) The nature of the creature		
(iv) The nature of the forest		
Total of 4.		
Average length of pause between pupil answer and teacher response	0.6	seconds
Average length of pause between teacher question and pupil response	0.85	seconds

about the island but also to speak orally at length. She might then be disappointed to discover that, in this phase of the lesson at any rate, a typical answer was just one, two or three words long.

Qualitative analysis

If the principal purpose of the explanation is to bring out salient points about significant features of the island, so that children can compose an imaginative piece of writing, then to some degree the success of the explanation will lie in the extent to which the teacher has broadened their vision and extended their imagination. These are all *qualitative* judgements to do with the nature of what is being learned, so quantitative and qualitative judgements can be taken together. Such matters as to whether something is worthwhile, important, valuable, morally right, in good taste, appropriate to the child

concerned, sufficiently demanding on the intellect, or far-sighted, are matters of personal opinion and professional judgement, and cannot be resolved by quantities alone.

It is not possible to say that all closed questions are 'good' or 'bad'. It depends on the nature of them and the personal judgement someone makes in the circumstances. 'What is your name?' is a not especially demanding closed question. 'What is the formula of DNA?' is also a closed question, in that there is not a choice of answers, but the demands are on a vastly different plane. Similarly, 'Can you tell me the surname of someone you know?' is an open question requiring little imagination from the respondent, whereas 'What is the meaning of life?' or 'How can we abolish war?' are open questions of mind-blowing proportions.

A transcript alone cannot give the full flavour of the quality of an explanation. In the episode above, we cannot tell from the text whether the teacher, when she says 'No, it's Emma's turn', is very cross with the pupil trying to speak, or is making her point in a kindly manner. The observer saw it as the latter. We cannot tell, when the teacher asks for words to describe the forest, whether most pupils were thinking about the question and attempting to answer. They were, according to the observer. Nor is it always clear what meanings and significance the teacher or pupils attach to events. This can sometimes be elicited not just by live observation but by interviewing the participants to see how they perceived the process.

The observer of the lesson above commented on the teacher's and the pupils' enthusiasm, the pleasure the teacher showed at pupils' answers, the generally high level of contribution from pupils, the discriminating manner in which the teacher responded to pupils' ideas, and the way later on, when they began to write, pupils were encouraged to develop their own ideas. The teacher said in interview that she wanted to give them somewhere to start, that was her main intention: 'They need a starting point. Once they have this their story can take them anywhere.' When the essays of this particular group of children were scored by two independent markers as part of the Leverhulme Primary Project research, they obtained some of the highest scores recorded, compared with other matched groups of children with different teachers engaged in the same explanation of the same island.

One fruitful way of analysing qualitative aspects of an explanation is to use the *'critical events'* approach. In order to do this you need to observe someone teaching and to select a period when some kind of explanation is taking place. You then select some event, it need not be spectacular, which seems in your judgement to help or impede children's understanding. This might be a neat analogy, a piece of factually incorrect information, a moment of sudden enlightenment, a well-composed sequence of questions, a failure to clarify someone's confusion, or some other significant happening. Follow the procedures described in Activity 7, filling in the spaces.

Levels of thought

One common way of analysing explanations is to look at the sort of thinking in which the pupils are being asked to engage. Numerous researchers have designed schedules for such analysis, and not every research instrument is suitable for use by teachers analysing their own lessons. Some are extremely complex and require lengthy training. Others have

a focus which might be of limited interest to many teachers, concentrating perhaps on the explanation of scientific concepts.

Many of these approaches have been influenced by Bloom's *Taxonomy of Educational Objectives* (Bloom *et al.* 1956). Bloom and his colleagues tried to devise a structure that would cover objectives for different levels of thinking, and he described six general categories based on a *hierarchical* view of thinking in classrooms. A hierarchical view assumes that higher levels of thought are based on, or make some use of, what is in the lower levels. His six major groupings were, in ascending order of level:

1 knowledge

2 comprehension

3 application

4 analysis

5 synthesis

6 evaluation

In order to *comprehend*, it was argued, you must have *knowledge*. To be able to *synthesize*, you will need to be able to *analyse*.

There have been many modifications of Bloom's *Taxonomy*, including some which have created extra classes, or evolved very specific sub-headings of the major categories. Brown and his colleagues (Brown *et al.* 1968) extended the category *analysis* to include such abilities as:

- distinguish fact from opinion;
- distinguish relevant from irrelevant information;
- detect error in thinking;
- infer purposes, points of view, thoughts, feelings;
- recognize bias or propaganda.

One of the most interesting outcomes of that particular view of children's thinking was the work of Hilda Taba and her associates at San Francisco State College. She believed that teachers could learn to move children up to higher levels of thinking, provided they knew how to analyse the relevant processes in the classroom. She concentrated in particular on the explaining of concepts, and on children, making inferences and applying principles. Her emphasis was on learning what to focus on, and then embarking on a set of steps that would extend and lift children's thinking through teachers and children both giving and seeking information.

Taba's thought levels were as follows:

0 Incorrect information;

1 Specific items of data;

ⓐ ACTIVITY 7

A critical event

1 What led up to the event?

2 What actually happened?

3 What was the outcome?

4 Interview the teacher and, if the teacher agrees, one or two of the pupils.

5 Compare your 'critical event' and the responses to it with the observations of others in your group, if possible.

Note: When interviewing the teacher and the pupils, use as neutrally worded an opening as possible, like, 'Can you tell me a bit about what happened when Jane asked you about crops in hot countries?' (to the teacher), or 'Can you tell me a bit about what happened when you asked the teacher about crops in hot countries?' (to the pupil). Avoid 'leading' questions such as, 'Why did you say "…" to that bright girl?' or 'Why did you look so puzzled when the teacher said "…"?'

2 Relating, comparing, contrasting items of data;
3 Factual explanation, or factual support of prediction;
4 Inferences from units of data, predictions;
5 Inferential logic;
6 Generalization from inferences.

Children were encouraged to move up to higher levels as they studied topics like 'The Pioneers'. Thus, a level-1 statement by a child would be, 'Sometimes the wagons got stuck in the snow' (specific item of data). A level-2 piece of thinking, which involved comparing and contrasting, would be 'Well, the pioneers weren't travelling on the ocean, like the colonists, they were travelling on just land.' Higher levels, according to Taba, would be achieved when children were helped to make inferences or generalizations from these. An example she gave of level 5, inferential logic, was, 'I'd rather have been with the colonists, because if I was a pioneer, I'd have had to walk all those miles and I don't think my feet would ever feel the same.' A level-6 statement would be, 'The witch doctors

are trying to do with wands and cracked eggs what our doctors do with needles', showing the child making a generalization from inferences.

There is no clear-cut research evidence that this approach to raising levels of thinking actually led to 'better' learning or to children scoring higher on tests of achievement (Dunkin and Biddle 1974), but the main interest is for teachers to be able to reflect on the *nature* of the thinking and learning that takes place as a result of their explanations. Many teachers have an intuitive belief, even if it is not always easy to prove empirically, that it is *desirable* for children to learn to think in different ways, some of which are arguably on a 'higher' plane than recalling facts alone. It is a topic, therefore, that is worthy of some careful scrutiny.

Pupils explaining

We have tried to point out on several occasions that explaining is not a one-way process. It is not solely a means for teachers to give something to pupils, hence the many examples we have quoted of interactive explanations, where both teacher and pupils ask questions or give information. It is too easy, when analysing teaching, to focus on the teacher alone and ignore the pupils, except when they answer questions. Yet children often can and do explain things to one another in class. Sometimes they are able to empathize with a fellow learner at a similar stage and use the right language or examples to make the point clearly, though one should not pretend that it is always like this.

It is well worth the time and effort involved to encourage children, from the first time you take them, to teach one another. Learning to explain a concept to another pupil, for example, serves two important functions. The first is that the child practises clear communication and thinks about the audience, even if this is only one person; the second is that explaining to someone else can often clarify your own ideas, or reveal what it is that you do not yourself fully understand. There are many examples of a pupil trying to explain something to another pupil and then calling in the teacher to help clarify a particular point, as in the following exchange between two pupils, one showing the other how to make a small kite out of wood veneer strip and tissue paper:

Pupil 1: You have to glue these two strips together ... no (pointing to two strips of wood veneer) not like that – in a cross shape.
Pupil 2: Where's the glue?
Pupil 1: Trevor's got it. Don't get it on the tissue paper or it won't fly.
Pupil 2: How long does this strip have to be?
Pupil 1: You put one strip downwards and then the other strip across it, like a cross.
Pupil 2: Yes, but what if you put two of the same together, what if this across piece is the same length as the down bit, will it still fly? I bet it'll crash.
Pupil 1: I'll ask miss. Miss! What happens if these two bits of wood are the same length? Will it crash?

Miss did not actually know and suggested they try it and find out, but we shall return to teachers' knowledge of subject matter in Unit 4.

ACTIVITY 8

1 Give children in your class the opportunity to explain something to one another. Set up an activity where you explain something to one member of a pair or a group, who must then, in turn, explain it to the others. It could be a simple piece of gymnastics in a PE lesson, instructions on how to do a maths problem, or a design and technology activity like designing a kite or making the tortoise, described earlier on page 14.

2 Eavesdrop discreetly on some of the 'explanations' as they occur around the room.

3 Make brief notes under the following headings:

Clarity (Is the explanation generally clear to the other pupil(s)?)

Language (Does the explainer use appropriate language?)

Examples (Does the pupil give an example or demonstration?)

Organization (Bearing in mind the age of the child, is it well organized?)

Learning (Do both explainer and other(s) appear to have learned something?)

4 Discuss your findings with the pupils concerned and, in a sensitive manner, with the class. What can you do to improve children's skill at explaining?

Using schedules

Many teachers prefer to analyse their own thinking by reflecting on it, rather than by writing notes. Sometimes, however, it can be useful to have a written account of an explanation, either a self-critique or a set of notes compiled by an observer. This can be particularly useful for initial trainees, when tutors and supervising teachers can offer the student a written version of their analysis. It can

Children explaining

also be valuable during the classroom observation parts of teacher appraisal. If the emphasis of lesson analysis is to improve the quality of teaching, then a written account can be a positive step towards this goal.

Often a freehand account is preferable, as the observer can react to events as they occur and then, after the lesson, discuss any notes made, leaving a copy for the teacher's own use. Sometimes people prefer more structure and may find a rating schedule, or a lesson observation proforma, more helpful.

Rating schedules must be used with care. They are best employed by experienced observers who have seen many teachers at work and have some idea of the range of skills to be seen in many primary classrooms, not just a single one. Often five-or seven-point scales are featured with 1 indicating 'weak' and 5 or 7 meaning 'excellent'. A typical rating schedule for analysing and commenting on explanations in a lesson or series of lessons, might look like this:

Sometimes it is helpful, with certain explanations, to draw a diagram showing what the key ideas will be and how they will relate and be linked. This can be done both by the teacher *before* the lesson and by the observer *during* the lesson, to see how the links seem to work out in practice.

Another approach is to use a scale of frequency, like 'always/usually/sometimes/once/never'. This would only give a frequency of events, in itself relatively limited, so a qualitative comment section is essential, otherwise the categories could be too limited. An example of this approach is shown in

Typical rating schedule for analysing explanations

Circle the appropriate number: 7 represents 'truly outstanding' teaching, 1 indicates 'a weak point', 4 is average for someone with your experience.

Explanations

1 Your explanations were clearly understood by the pupils.   1 2 3 4 5 6 7

2 Your explanations covered the essential points.   1 2 3 4 5 6 7

3 The examples, analogies and illustrations you gave were appropriate to the topic/activity.   1 2 3 4 5 6 7

4 You listened to children's responses.   1 2 3 4 5 6 7

5 You clarified children's responses where necessary.   1 2 3 4 5 6 7

6 You made effective use of teaching aids where appropriate.   1 2 3 4 5 6 7

7 You made effective use of your voice.   1 2 3 4 5 6 7

Usually such a schedule would also contain a 'Comments' section, allowing the observer to make specific remarks about, for example, factual accuracy and the quality of demonstrations, if these were appropriate, and such matters as movement or gesture, where these amplified explanations.

Sometimes a more sharply focused schedule or outline will be helpful if you want to concentrate on analysing and improving a particular aspect of explaining. Suppose, for example, you wanted to improve the clarity of your explanation by making the central keys or ideas more distinct and more effectively linked. In that case, a format like the one on p. 29 might be helpful. The keys or main ideas are filled in in the centre boxes *before* the lesson by the teacher, and the observer then makes notes about the teacher's and pupils' use of language in the left-hand and right-hand boxes.

Activity 9, which is a paired activity. It can be done by two teachers, two students, or a student and a teacher working reciprocally.

ⓐ ACTIVITY 9

1 Use the observation schedule on p. 28 in another teacher's or student's lessons.

2 Ask the other person to observe you using the same observation schedule.

3 Discuss each other's lessons and both your observations.

4 Consider how you can improve your own explaining skill.

Note to observer: tick whichever box you judge as appropriate in each case. Some aspects will not be seen often, and your comments will clarify the category chosen.

	Always	Usually	Sometimes	Once	Never	COMMENTS
Clear introduction	☐	☐	☐	☐	☐	
New terms clarified	☐	☐	☐	☐	☐	
Apt word choice	☐	☐	☐	☐	☐	
Clear sentence structure	☐	☐	☐	☐	☐	
Vagueness avoided	☐	☐	☐	☐	☐	
Adequate concrete examples	☐	☐	☐	☐	☐	
Within pupils' experience	☐	☐	☐	☐	☐	
Voice used to emphasize	☐	☐	☐	☐	☐	
Emphasis by gestures	☐	☐	☐	☐	☐	
Appropriate pauses	☐	☐	☐	☐	☐	
Direct verbal cueing	☐	☐	☐	☐	☐	
Repetition used	☐	☐	☐	☐	☐	
Main ideas paraphrased	☐	☐	☐	☐	☐	
Sound use of media, materials	☐	☐	☐	☐	☐	
Pattern of explanation clear	☐	☐	☐	☐	☐	
Parts linked to each other	☐	☐	☐	☐	☐	
Progressive summary	☐	☐	☐	☐	☐	
Pace or level altered	☐	☐	☐	☐	☐	
Opportunity for pupil questions	☐	☐	☐	☐	☐	
Grasp of main ideas checked	☐	☐	☐	☐	☐	
Pupil commitment sought	☐	☐	☐	☐	☐	

Observation schedule for explaining

Format for analysis of key ideas in explanation

Observer's notes on features of teacher's language use	IDEAS OR 'KEYS' BEING EXPLAINED (To be filled in by the teacher before the lesson)	Observer's notes on features of pupils' language use

Unit 4

KNOWING THE SUBJECT MATTER

Part of any successful explanation, particularly of a concept or an idea, is accurate and correct presentation of the relevant knowledge. There is no point in being a brilliant exponent of the art of explaining and then filling children's heads with incorrect information and dreary ideas, or equipping them with low level skills when they and the teacher are capable of better. Consider this transcript from a lesson on insects observed during the Leverhulme Primary Project:

Teacher: I'm going to give you the little word 'insect'. Immediately in your mind there's a picture of something, I expect. There is in mine. What sort of picture have you got Cassandra?

Pupil 1: A spider.

Teacher: OK, you think of a spider. You keep the spider there. Peter, what about you?

Pupil 2: (No response)

Teacher: When I say 'insect' what do you immediately think of – an insect? . . . What is an insect? . . . Tell me the name of an insect.

Pupil 3: A ladybird.

Teacher: Yes, that's right.

Pupil 4: A worm.

Teacher: Yes. Anything else?

Pupil 3: A snail.

Teacher: That's right, a snail's an insect. How do insects move around? Peter?

Pupil 2: Legs.

Teacher: How many legs has an insect got?

Pupil 2: Six.

Teacher: Yes, six, but do insects get around any other way?

Pupil 2: Some insects fly.

Teacher: Yes, some insects use wings. Can you think of an insect that flies?

Pupil 2: An eagle.

Teacher: An eagle? Is that an insect? No, it's a bird.

A bird is definitely not an insect.

(Later, at the end of the episode)

Teacher: So we've thought about a whole set of different insects today: snails, centipedes, ladybirds, caterpillars and woodlice, and we've also found a lot of ways in which these insects move about – crawling, walking, sliding, swimming, flying and hopping.

At the end of this explanation, children were given a test in which they had to identify insects and then describe them in more detail. The children in this group obtained very low scores, and it is not too difficult to see why. To some extent the ineffectiveness of the episode can be explained by several of the points discussed in earlier units in this book: lack of distinct 'keys' as the explanation fuses examples of insects with their method of movement, but not their salient characteristics; lack of clarity in general, with confusion over such matters as legs, when the teacher accepts that insects have six legs, but also agrees that a worm and a snail are insects.

The most stridently obvious defect of the explanation, however, is that the teacher himself does not know what an insect's characteristics actually are. Indeed, he is simply wrong in much of the information he gives the class. By incorrectly accepting 'spider' as the very first response from Cassandra, he sows doubt in the minds of those who perhaps knew something about insects, and these uncertainties are compounded when snails, worms, centipedes and other unlikely candidates are allowed to join the insect club unchallenged. At the end of the explanation, insects, to these children, seem to be anything smallish that crawls, swims, flies or hops around, other than birds. The true

Mastering different kinds of subject matter

concept 'insect' is never communicated. Almost all the teachers observed during our research gave much clearer and more factually accurate explanations than this one.

Different kinds of subject matter?

The professional expertise of people who have become masters of different kinds of subject matter can consist of many elements. Mastery involves more than the mere mechanical acquisition of certain factual information, though having a formidable body of knowledge is a central requisite. Those who have mastered a particular subject or profession will usually have acquired:

- a significant body of knowledge;
- an understanding of the major and many minor concepts central to the subjects;
- an understanding of the structure of the subject and a desire to learn more about it.

Take a subject like music as an example. Professional musicians will have a considerable grasp of, usually, a wide range of musical knowledge, from simple concepts of notation up to an intimate knowledge of numerous symphonies, concertos, operas, songs and other types of music. They will have the skill to play certain instruments at a very high standard of proficiency, to sing, to compose, to conduct, to score, to improvise. They will also usually have a lifelong interest in music which leads them to broaden and extend their repertoire, improve their playing or singing, or create new compositions, throughout their career.

There is, however, a significant difference between those who are able to master one single discipline and primary teachers. In present-day primary schools most teachers, unless their teaching is confined to one subject, are expected to have some familiarity with a body of subject matter so broad that no one on earth could more than scratch the surface of it, let alone master it. Those who are generalist primary teachers may be expected to know about physical and biological sciences, earth science, technology, literature, the arts, physical education, the humanities and numerous forms of interdisciplinary study. It is a formidable list.

One of the present writers was once teaching a class of 6 and 7 year olds. The topic was 'The World around Us' and pupils were invited to ask questions about their own immediate environment. In the first 30 seconds this group of children of modest ability asked: 'Why are cars made of metal?', 'Why does smoke come out of the back of a motor bike?', 'Why does it snow?' and 'Why does a wagtail wag its tail?' It was nothing that a couple of lifetimes in the nearest multi-media library could not have solved, but most of us are as competent to handle the more searching questions asked by children as to perform a piece of triple bypass surgery.

Knowledge of subject matter and strategies for explaining are often closely connected. If you have a good grasp of the content (i.e. *what* is to be taught), it puts you in a better position to determine appropriate strategies (i.e. *how* to explain the topic), though mastery of subject matter does not actually guarantee clear exposition. Some knowledgeable people, paralysed by the complexity of what they know, are not able to communicate and empathize with those in possession of less knowledge. The lack of knowledge about insects shown by the teacher in the preceding extract was a distinct handicap to clear exposition, simply because he did not know what the main teaching points about insects were, so he could not map them out in his mind or in his planning.

Different topics involve different kinds of subject matter. In order to explain to a class how to use a microelectronics kit, why certain materials are better than others when designing and constructing something, who the Tudors were, how to calculate the area of a triangle, or what erosion is, teachers need to possess, or have access to, considerable bodies of the relevant subject matter. But explaining about the quality of writing in a book; or how people deal with moral dilemmas; or the impact on the emotions of a poem, painting, or piece of music; or the spirit in which team games should be played, involves a mixture of factual content, judgements about values, the intelligence of feeling, and a degree of imagination.

Explanations, where part of the 'subject matter' requires use of the imagination, pose an interesting problem. If the teacher prescribes too much in advance, then both children's and teacher's imagination could be inhibited. Yet a certain amount

of explaining and exploring must take place.

ⓐ ACTIVITY 10

1 Look at the map of the Island of Zarg on page 21. Plan a lesson for a group of children in which you will explore ideas with them prior to their doing a piece of writing about the island.

2 Teach the lesson with the class and ask them to write a story entitled 'My Adventure on the Island of Zarg'. Make a tape or video recording of the lesson, if possible.

3 Read and mark the children's stories and discuss these with them.

4 Consider the following questions:
   (i) *What was the nature and structure of your lesson?*
   How did you introduce the island?
   What seemed to be the main ideas or keys – features of the island? children's feelings? creating a sense of mystery? excitement? curiosity? the bizarre or unusual? How did these evolve? Were they linked?
   (ii) *What strategies did you employ?*
   What did you tell the children?
   What sort of questions did you ask?
   What additional aids did you use – music? pictures?
   Did you use drama, or role play?
   (iii) *What did the children do?*
   Were they active or passive?
   How did they respond to the main ideas and keys?
   What did they initiate themselves?
   How did their contributions and ideas affect the development of the lesson?
   (iv) *What was the written work like?*
   Did it appear to have been influenced by the activities that preceded it? If so, in what way? If not, why not?
   Was the written response what you expected?
   What particularly pleased you? What disappointed you?
   What did the children say to you about the activity and their own writing?
   Did they seem to have found it an interesting and absorbing assignment?
   Did you detect any development in the quality of their written work, however small?
   (v) *How did you assess the writing?*
   What features of the writing did you

particularly value?

What did you do about spelling, punctuation, grammatical or syntactical errors?

What sort of explaining did you do when you handed work back to the children?

5 In the light of your experience of teaching the lesson, of listening to and viewing it on tape, and, if you had the opportunity, of discussing it with the children, and with an observer if that was possible, of reading the children's writing, and reflecting on the whole thing, how would you improve what you did? See if you can do a similar exercise with a different group.

Explaining concepts

Learning subject matter often involves mastering a set of concepts. These can be of several kinds. Some of the salient ones can be said to be the 'keys' which, when linked, lead to understanding, as we mentioned earlier. Like big pieces in a young child's jigsaw puzzle, put them together in the right way and you may have a picture of the whole thing. Some concepts are tiny and precise, others are large and diffuse, open to different interpretations. The concept 'happiness', for example, may have quite different features in the eyes of an eskimo, a child, a millionaire and a Trappist monk, but what is in common is that their individual versions of it give them pleasure or satisfaction.

There are four essential features which need to be considered when explaining concepts. These are:

1 **Label or name** The actual word(s) used to name the concept – 'crops', 'reptile', 'electricity', 'harmony', 'colour', 'monarchy', 'ambition'.

2 **Attributes** These are of two kinds:
   (i) *must have* – features which are essential parts of the concept, indeed criteria in its definition, like 'wings' (bird), 'having a grandchild' (grandparents), 'eagerness to succeed' (ambition);
   (ii) *may have* – features which occur in certain cases, but are not prerequisites, like 'brown coloured' birds (applies to sparrows and thrushes, but not to every bird), 'retired' grandparents (many are still working), 'seeking wealth' in ambitious people (some may seek power and scorn wealth).

3 **Examples** These are also of two kinds:
   (i) *illustrative examples* – actual cases which meet the criteria, such as 'robin' (bird), 'Mr and Mrs Scroggins' (grandparents), 'seeking out influential people to further one's career' (ambition);
   (ii) *not-examples* – cases which do not meet the criteria, but then, by comparison, illustrate what the real criteria for inclusion in the concept actually are, such as 'dragon-fly' (flies, but is not a bird), 'Mr and Mrs Bloggs' (elderly, but not grandparents), 'obtaining promotion' (often the result of ambition, but could also happen to the unambitious).

4 **Rules** – The full definition listing the 'must have' attributes and their relationship to each other.

If we were to map out the familiar concept 'Insects' according to this scheme, it would look like this:

Subject area	Science (*subdivisions* – biology – zoology)
Name	Insect
Attributes	(i) *must have* – six legs, head, thorax, abdomen, two antennae, wings
	(ii) *may have* – a woodland habitat, a black or brown body, stripes, a beautiful appearance, a liking for fruit, a smooth shell, hairy legs.
Examples	(i) *illustrative examples* – house-fly, beetle, butterfly, wasp, ladybird
	(ii) *not-examples* – spider (arachnid), scorpion (arachnid), snail (gastropod), woodlouse (isopod land crustacean).
Rules	Insects have six legs, a head, thorax and abdomen, two antennae and two or four wings.

Another valuable use of 'not-examples' is to clarify what the true attributes of the concept are. By comparing a honeycomb, a chessboard or a crossword puzzle, where the shapes do 'tessellate' – that is, fit together in a regular pattern – with what happens when you try to press differently sized circles or most star shapes together, where they will not meet all round, the concept 'tessellation' becomes clearer.

Looking at the 'not-examples' and 'may have' attributes can also help avoid stereotyping, as well as aid the development of more rigorous thinking in children. Stereotyping is, on occasion, a biological lifesaver. If we stay well away from all snakes, simply because some are poisonous, then this will help us avoid being bitten by those that are venomous. Stereotyping is the acquisition of a fixed mental attitude to something on the basis of one or more characteristics. But it is an oversimplification that is sometimes, indeed it can often be, incorrect, though it is related to accommodating the environment. In childhood, for example, most of us are at some time stung by a bee or a wasp. We then stereotype all black-and-yellow striped insects as likely to sting and therefore to be avoided, yet many are completely harmless and enjoy, as a result of their colouring, some immunity from predators. If a teacher were explaining the concept 'Ruritanian', then the only definition of it may be 'those born in, or naturalized as residents of, Ruritania'. But if children have met or read about a Ruritanian who is lazy, violent or dishonest, they may generalize this 'may have' attribute to all Ruritanians and wrongly stereotype them.

 ACTIVITY 11

1 Choose two key concepts which you are likely to need to explain to a class, a group or an individual. Select one which is fairly specific and definable, like 'mammal', 'island', or 'the Romans', and one which is more diffuse and difficult to pin down, such as 'progress', 'a good building' or 'great music'.

2 Map out each of the two according to the scheme suggested above with attributes, examples and rules.

3 Explain the concept to a group of children, or even to an individual. See what strategies and teaching aids you need to make the concept clear – a video of *Question Time* or part of a debate in Parliament? A drawing of an island or a map? Photographs of various buildings? A tape of different kinds of music so children can discuss what constitutes 'great' music?

4 Evaluate to what extent your 'map' of the concept helped in the exposition of it.

Written explanations

Teachers are not the sole sources of information available to pupils. In addition to pictures, videos, tapes, slides, videodiscs, broadcast television and radio, there is a wide variety of print material – books, worksheets, pamphlets, newspapers, magazines and the printed word parts of pictures or diagrams. Many of the acts of explaining in which teachers find themselves engaged are related to

printed text, a worksheet, perhaps, which has been compiled by the teacher, or a textbook published commercially.

Much of what has been learned about explanations in textbooks is of relevance to what is covered in this book. Explanations of critical subject matter and key concepts can be clouded, both in textbooks and classroom teaching, by such factors as lack of clarity, inappropriate language, poor links between ideas, or inaccuracy. In some cases the presence of one or two technical words or phrases may make a text difficult, and teachers may often have to explain these so that children can cope with a text which otherwise may not be too difficult for them.

 ACTIVITY 12

1 Read this passage and then answer the questions below:

Timefrittoons

Most people have at least one timefrittoon. Many of us have several and some people acquire more as they get older. Erdgraben is a common timefrittoon, and it can be quite geldverlangend, though older people often have to make it ungeldverlangend. One elderly man devotes every single day to his timefrittoon. He doesn't mind that erdgraben can be a dirty timefrittoon. 'I don't find it very geldverlangend at all,' he said recently, 'my cousin's timefrittoon is quite a bit more geldverlangend than mine and nowhere near as healthy.'

(i)   Give the names of three timefrittoons.
(ii)   Which is likely to be the most geldverlangend?
(iii) Can erdgraben sometimes be a dirty timefrittoon?
(iv)   Are all dogs healthy?
(v)   Write a short essay on 'Timefrittoons in the 21st Century'.

2 What do you think the passage is about? How well did you answer the questions? You were probably able to answer some of them without even understanding the passage. For example, you could answer (i) in part, because the text tells you that erdgraben is a timefrittoon; the answer to (iii) is also given in the passage, because erdgraben can be dirty; you could have answered (iv) without even reading the passage, because it is quite clear that all dogs are not healthy (the

mention of dogs is a distractor, it has nothing to do with the passage) and you may have been able to waffle on about the essay in (v) with a bit of deft footwork. 'Correct' answers to questions do not always guarantee understanding.

3 If you were a pupil, you would probably want your teacher to explain three unfamiliar terms to you – *timefrittoon*, *erdgraben* and *geldverlangend/ungeldverlangend* – so that you could understand the passage properly. So now read the text again, in the knowledge that timefrittoons are 'hobbies', erdgraben is 'gardening' and geldverlangend/ungeldverlangend is 'expensive/inexpensive'.

4 Take a textbook or worksheet you are using with a group of children and identify any words or phrases that you think might cause them difficulties. Ask some of the children to tell you which terms they do not understand. Are your lists the same? Try explaining the terms to the children. Read up some of the work on text readability (Harrison 1980).

Coping strategies

As part of the Leverhulme Primary Project we conducted a number of studies of primary teachers' own subject knowledge and the gaps in it. One of our surveys of several hundred teachers showed that teachers felt *most* competent to teach English and maths, but *least* well equipped in science, music and technology. Even within a field like science there can be wide differences, and three-quarters of teachers felt able to teach 'the water cycle' with their existing subject knowledge, but only one-sixth said they could teach microelectronics without extra help.

When we studied teachers explaining subjects in science like 'electricity', 'floating and sinking' and

Explaining electrical circuits

'levers', we found that the most difficult problem was coping with unpredicted events or with children's questions. If a group could not make the bulb light up in an electrical circuit, many teachers felt they were unable to help. When asked why an orange floats with its peel on, but sinks when peeled, or why most sand sinks, but some grains stay on the surface, many teachers did not have the necessary grasp of such concepts as 'density', 'surface tension' or 'Archimedes' Principle' which would be necessary for an explanation of some of the phenomena associated with floating and sinking.

We found that teachers used various strategies for coping with their own lack of knowledge, including frank admission (one teacher began a lesson on electrical circuits with, 'Look, I have to be honest with you. I know nothing about electricity. I can just about change a fuse'), occasionally evasion, sometimes an offer to find out, more often an invitation to the children to find out for themselves.

There are several reasons why teachers need to learn to devise strategies for when they are explaining unfamiliar subject matter. There could be a safety issue (gymnastics, use of cutting tools); teachers who appear to know little may eventually lose respect; continued personal growth is an important part of teachers' professional development. Lack of sound subject knowledge can also affect teaching strategies. For example, if you don't know what a capacitor is, in a lesson in microelectronics, you may not be able to think up an appropriate analogy, like, 'A capacitor introduces a delay in the circuit, so when you switch on, the bulb won't light up immediately. There will be a short delay with a small capacitor and a bigger delay with a big capacitor. It's a bit like a bucket filling up with water. A little bucket will soon fill up and then overflow, but a bigger bucket will take longer.'

Most of the teachers we interviewed wanted *people* to help them. Some used the school's specialist (maths, science, etc.) co-ordinators, others used a teachers' centre, a spouse, or a governor; one even used a parent who was a science graduate. Think of the following possibilities, in your own case, should you find yourself on unfamiliar ground:

- *People* who can help: a fellow teacher, a friend, someone on a 'help' line, a librarian, an adviser;
- *Books*: encyclopedias, library sources, dictionaries, specialist texts;
- *Multi-media*: videos, tapes, pictures, videodisc, broadcast radio and television.

Finally, reflect on these events and consider how you would react if they were to occur in your classroom. You could avoid the issue (not fair, if you can manage to help, you should); you might ask the child to find out for him- or herself (but help is needed: a suggestion of a book, dictionary or source of information like the library or a database); you could promise to find out for another day (but you need to honour this promise, otherwise children feel let down); you might ask a group of people to find out (but again, help is needed – who does what? and where?); you could try to find out jointly with the children ('I'll write to X, you write to Y').

ACTIVITY 13

What would you do if the following occurred?

1 Someone asks you, 'Who were the Aztecs, exactly?'

2 You see a pupil cutting something in a technology lesson and feel there is some danger, even though the pupil is being sensible.

3 In a project lesson on 'Our Village', you are asked 'When was our village founded?'

4 A 6 year old asks you, 'Does God ever die?'

5 Someone brings in a radio kit and asks you to explain how a transistor works.

6 You have to introduce a project on 'Energy'.

7 You are asked to teach a class to sing a song in two-part harmony for the school concert.

8 You are asked to do some paintings with children which are composed of dots and blotches, 'pointillist' style.

EFFECTIVE EXPLAINING

There are many different ways of considering what kind of teaching is 'effective'. For some people, effectiveness means carrying out whatever the teacher intended to carry out. In order to find out whether this was the case, some argue that children should be given a test, whereby 'success' will be judged according to how well pupils score on the test. But critics of this approach say that tests measure only a limited amount of what has been learned. Consequently, judgements about effectiveness are often made on the basis of several sources of information. These include test scores; other assessments of pupil learning; professional judgement by someone competent to appraise classroom teaching; self-appraisal by the teacher; opinions of others thought to be competent to judge, like heads of schools, fellow teachers, children themselves. In practice, it is not usually possible, or even desirable, to subject a teacher to all these forms of review at once. In this unit, therefore, we shall concentrate on pupil learning, self-appraisal, classroom strategies, and some of the research on effective explaining. We shall begin by reviewing some of the points made earlier in this book.

Main features of effective explaining

Clarity

Nate Gage (1968) put this in a nutshell:

> some people explain aptly, getting to the heart of the matter with just the right terminology, examples and organization of ideas. Other explainers, on the contrary, get us and themselves all mixed up, use terms beyond our level of comprehension, draw inept analogies

Clarity, therefore, includes some of the following features:

1 *Clear structure* The 'keys' or central ideas are distinct and the essence of them, attributes, concepts, whatever, is made clear. There are links between the main ideas and these give the whole explanation coherence and a logical shape. There is a clearly set out opening and, where necessary, a closing review or summary from the teacher, the pupils or book.

2 *Clear language* The choice of words and phrases are apt for both the topic and the child or children concerned being neither too banal, nor at too high a level of abstraction. In other words, the linguistic *register* is appropriate and the words are well chosen.

3 *Clear Voice* The voice is well modulated with light and shade, not pitched at a fixed level of monotony. The voice is amplified by gesture and movement, emphasis, facial expression and animation, as is suitable in the circumstances.

4 *Fluency* Clarity is maintained by fluency. The explanation flows at the sort of pace that holds the attention rather than allows a lapse into tedium. Genuine enthusiasm and interest by the teacher can help stimulate flow.

Strategies

Explaining is not a one-way process. It is not merely a question of someone who knows something drumming it into the head of someone who does not. Hence a wide range of strategies may be effective. These include the following:

1 *Questioning* Using appropriate questions to see how much children already know, to discover what they understand, to review what they have learned, to reflect the higher or lower order of thinking which is necessary.

2 *Use of examples/analogies* Choosing or eliciting illustrative examples and 'not-examples',

analogies and 'not-analogies', anecdotes or stories, appropriate to the level of intellectual development of the child or group.

3 *Use of practical work* Selection or endorsement (if ideas come from pupils) of practical work and activities which enhance understanding.

4 *Use of teaching aids* Using a range of pictorial or other materials, images and sounds that involve several of the senses to reinforce or amplify the explanatory process, varying the stimulus sensitively.

5 *Management/organization* Arranging discussion, activities, movement and seating so that optimum conditions for learning and understanding are established and a high degree of attentiveness and involvement is maintained. Such matters as these and notions like 'eye contact' are covered in the book on *Class Management* in this series (Wragg 1993).

Pupils' perspective

The purpose of an explanation is to give understanding to the learner. This aspect highlights several points that are relevant when the effectiveness of explaining is appraised. Indeed, ability to *empathize* with the learner is the hallmark of the effective explainer. The ability to see concepts, issues, processes from the learner's point of view means that choice of language, examples, points to emphasize, review questions and so on, will be more apt. A simple example is in the use of gesture. If you are explaining a set of figures that shows a *downward* trend, and if your audience is facing you, you would need to move your finger from high right to low left (Picture A on p. 40) as *you* see it, so that it comes over to *them* as high left to low right (Picture B on p. 41). If you demonstrate the trend from your own point of view, the class will see the movement the wrong way round. This is a banal example of empathy, perhaps, but it illustrates the principle of seeing what you are explaining from someone else's viewpoint.

Points to be borne in mind when talking of the pupil's perspective include:

1 *Understanding* During the explanatory process, children's understanding grows and the teacher should be able to predict the final expected level of attainment, given the capabilities of the child concerned.

2 *Involvement* Children should be involved in,

rather than being the passive recipients of an explanation, i.e. participating in discussion, asking and answering questions, making suggestions or observations and helping to shape the process, wherever this is appropriate. This is not to say that every explanation should be interactive, but that there should be sensitivity to the active role that children might play.

3 *Mutual explanation* Opportunities should be provided for children to explain to teachers, and for children to explain to one another.

4 *Listening* Teachers must listen to children and respond to what they hear, while children must listen to the teacher and to one another.

5 *Using and extending ideas* It is important to secure some degree of involvement, but a further step is to weave pupils' ideas into the discussion or activity and then extend these. One teacher we observed regularly built his explanations around pupils' proposals: 'Now Jennifer told us that if you mix red and blue paint you get purple, and Sam said that red and yellow make orange, and Allyson said that if you mix all of them together you get a "big mess"! So what do we mix to make a nice bright green colour?'

6 *Humour* There are many kinds of humour, and studies have shown that children like humour, though they dislike sarcasm. Humour related to the concept(s) being explained, as opposed to gratuitous humorous asides not relevant to the topic, may help learning, as it can aid recall and, in certain cases, enhance understanding. Humour should appear natural and spontaneous, as forced humour can have a much less positive effect.

7 *Further appetite* Try to create a feeling that something interesting and worthwhile has been learned and an appetite for learning more.

Discover or be told?

There are numerous arguments about which kinds of approach in teaching are the most effective. One of the most frequent issues to be debated is about discovery learning and didactic teaching, where the emphasis in the former is on children finding out for themselves, and in the latter on teachers telling pupils. Within the teaching profession there is much more tolerance of diversity than outside it. Most teachers recognize that it is common practice to vary one's strategies and styles according to circumstance, so that a teacher may give information directly on one occasion and encourage children to explore a topic on another.

As the teacher sees it (Picture A)

Often in the mass media, however, the assumption is that teachers are in two fiercely opposed camps, 'traditional' and 'progressive'. Yet in the fifth century BC, Confucius described in his *Analects* how he capitalized on the urge to discover: 'If out of the four corners of a subject I have dealt thoroughly with one corner and the pupils cannot then find out the other three for themselves, then I do not explain any more.'

Discovery, related as it is to the satisfying of curiosity – a powerful drive in primary age children – can be highly motivating. When young children learn for the first time that a magnet will pick up a paper clip, and that the paper clip will in turn, now that it is magnetized, pick up a second paper clip, they can be beside themselves with excitement. If someone simply told them this without either a demonstration or the opportunity to find out for themselves, the impact would be far weaker. On the negative side, discovery can be enormously time consuming, can sometimes lead to incorrect conclusions, and can follow numerous false trails. It could, in certain circumstances, be dangerous, for example if children were using cutting tools, exploring the environment, or engaging in quick physical movement.

Didactic teaching, direct information-giving, has the advantage of allowing the teacher to cover a great deal of ground quickly, to control the subject matter being learned, to make sure it is correct and based on what has been learned by previous generations, and to short-cut a lot of anguish. The negative side is that children may merely be able to reproduce notions and facts that are ill-understood. The process may have engendered no commitment or excitement.

The problem with polarizing this kind of debate is that it presupposes that there is no alternative to belonging to one extreme or the other. Many teachers are able to set up conditions whereby children discover things that, to experienced adults, are predictable. No well-informed adult will be

As the children see it (Picture B)

surprised to know that a strong magnet can pick up a whole chain of loose paper clips, so 'discovery' can also take place in a well-structured environment.

A programme of teaching based entirely on unstructured discovery would be disastrous. If every generation of children had to find out for itself how to solve quadratic equations, that water consisted of two atoms of hydrogen and one of oxygen, that penicillin can cure certain infections, or how to build a suspension bridge or an aircraft, then progress would occur only very slowly, if at all. What has been learned by previous generations can be used as a basis on which present and future generations can build. Collecting, analysing, synthesizing and communicating the accumulated wisdom of the world is a vital task in our civilization. Yet no one can know all there is to know, so being able to find out for yourself, and discover novelties, alone or with others, is also a vital skill in our society.

In this context, explaining takes on different forms: when *telling* someone, the teacher takes the lead, structures the information, sequences it, selects the examples, makes the summary; when *discovery* is stressed, then pupils are expected to share in the shaping of the explanation, as some matters they will explain to themselves or each other, and certain issues they will bring to the teacher for an explanation. Here is a little 'experiment' you can try in order to see how children respond to approaches that involve discovery, or being told, or a mixture.

a ACTIVITY 14

1 It is worth trying out two or three different approaches occasionally, not solely to see which is arguably more 'effective' in the context, but to see what is the outcome of contrasting styles of explanation. Try to teach each 'method' with

equal enthusiasm and also with a group of comparable size and ability. Here are three suggestions:

(i) **Magnetism**

Method A: Tell a class of children about magnets. Do most of the talking yourself.

Method B: Select a dozen different objects (as described on page 16). Explain to a group of children that they should put the objects into 'Yes' and 'No' piles, depending on whether or not they think a magnet will pick up each object (paper clip, plastic rod, perspex, copper, etc.). Then they should use their magnet to test out their theory and rearrange the piles if necessary.

Method C: Give each child a magnet. Ask them to discover what magnets will and won't pick up by any method they choose (i.e. you do *not* provide any objects or suggestions yourself). See what the outcome is and what conclusions they reach.

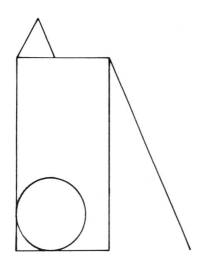

(ii) **Shapes**

Method A: Tell the group they must draw a diagram which contains a circle, a triangle, a rectangle and a line. You will describe it to them (but do *not* show them the diagram). Then tell them what to do, for example, 'Draw a tall rectangle about 2 inches across and 4 inches high ... now draw a small circle touching the left-hand and bottom lines ... draw a 1-inch triangle on top of ...', etc.

Method B: Begin as above, but tell the group that they must ask you questions about each of the four shapes – where they are, how big, what relationship they have to one another. So someone might ask, 'Where is the triangle?' or 'How big is the circle?'

(iii) **Island of Zarg**

Method A: Take the map of the Island of Zarg shown on page 21. Give each child a copy and then tell them about the main features on the island. Ask them to write a story called, 'My Adventure on the Island of Zarg'.

Method B: Give them the map of the Island of Zarg, but say nothing about it. Instead tell them they must, with a partner, spend 10 minutes looking at the map and discussing what it must be like on the island, and that then they should write a story entitled, 'My Adventure on the Island of Zarg'. Make it clear that they must *not* start writing their story immediately, but rather must first 'explore' the island with the other pupil.

2 Evaluate each of the approaches you have used, asking questions such as:

• How long was needed for each 'method'?
• Were some approaches more time-consuming than others?
• How clear, for each 'method', were children about what they had learned?
• How involved did children appear to be under each approach?
• What did children actually learn?
• What did they remember of each activity when you asked them about it one week later?

There are many variations you can invent for this kind of 'experiment'. It is an intuitive rather than a scientific method, giving you a chance to exercise professional judgement; however, the principal aim is to try out structured, semi-structured and unstructured or loosely structured approaches to see what works well. You might find, for example, that 'discovery' takes more time, but leads to more commitment and interest; alternatively, that 'telling' leads to the learning of correct information while 'discovery' leads to misconceptions. By trying different approaches with an open mind, you can widen your repertoire of professional skills, and also decide when and in what context it makes more sense to give information and when it is worth engaging in discovery. It would be a dreary teacher who did not do both at some time or other.

Effecting creativity?

Finally, in this unit, perhaps you might like to try a much more open-ended type of explanation, where it is by no means easy to determine effectiveness. In the case of many factual or conceptual types of explanation, it is fairly simple to ask, 'Did the child learn and understand the concept?' But not all explanations lend themselves to such a straightforward assessment of their effectiveness. In the arts, in creative writing, in certain aspects of humanities topics and in personal, social and moral education, what has been learned is not easy to measure. Activity 15 gives you the opportunity to try something open-ended and unpredictable and then try to evaluate it.

Helping children to become more 'creative' can seem a diffuse objective. What do we mean by 'creative'? How do we assess 'creativity'? What standards of judgement apply to a notion as vague-sounding as 'having creative ideas'? There are several possibilities you can try which involve skills of explaining that can go well beyond the routine and which challenge both teachers' and children's imagination. In Activity 15 it is important to encourage children to produce ideas, making sure that the nervous, who are often afraid to express their more unusual thoughts (in case people should laugh *at* them rather than *with* them), are given support and confidence. It is often the out-of-the-ordinary ideas that are the winners.

 ACTIVITY 15

1 Try one or more of the following 'creativity' exercises.
  (i) *Inventing new buttons*
      Tell the children that they are going to design hundreds of buttons. Draw a 10 x 10 chessboard shape on the board, leaving space for more than ten ideas on either side. Explain that children must suggest *shapes* for buttons (round, square, star-shaped, tree-shaped, etc.) and these will be written along the top. Next ask for *materials* for buttons: plastic, wood, metal, carrot (they have just invented the first edible button) or whatever children suggest. Each square of the chessboard shape thus contains a button idea, from the conventional 'round, plastic' to the more unusual 'flower-shaped, metal' to the way-out 'Great Britain-shaped, chocolate', depending on what has emerged. Look through all the ideas – some will be familiar (round, plastic) but some will be novel. Do not reject the offbeat ones out of hand.
  (ii) *Inventing new ice-creams*
      As in the buttons exercise, but substitute 'flavours' and 'add-ons' as the two dimensions, e.g. chocolate with nuts, vanilla with raisins, tomato with onion, etc.
  (iii) *Improving a toy*
      Take a cuddly toy rabbit, doll or teddy bear and ask the class to suggest ways to make it more fun to play with (make its ears/legs move, eyes light up, legs detachable, etc.).
  (iv) *What if?*
      Ask the class to discuss what would happen if the world were different in some way, for example, if we had two heads; if it rained so much the streets were always 1 foot deep in water; if it were always freezing; if we were 1 inch (or 20 feet) tall; if we had eyes at the end of each of our fingers.

2 Examine the way you 'explained' in these sessions. What was your response to unusual ideas? Could you handle them? Were you threatened by them? Did they make you laugh? Did you favour certain kinds of suggestion and feel less well disposed towards others? If so, which and why?

3 Look at the ideas the children produced. Did they appear to be safe, orthodox, wild, or inventive? To what extent did your own contribution shape the nature of the ideas being produced?

4 How can what you have learned from this exercise influence your explaining in a more orthodox context?

Inventing new buttons

FEEDBACK

One of the most important elements in skilful teaching, not solely in explaining, is being able to act on signals and messages about how effectively or ineffectively pupils are learning. Knowledge of results, or 'feedback' as it is commonly termed, can and should influence each stage of an explanation. For example, suppose you have to explain to children about a field trip to see some interesting geographical and ecological features at a seaside location. The complete explanation might include:

- *geographical features*: rock formations, fossils, cliffs, erosion;
- *ecology*: marine life, shellfish, seaweed, fish, birds;
- *commercial aspects*: fishing, tourism, harbour, coastland farming;
- *safety matters*: dangers of cliff falls, drowning, being cut off by tide;
- *logistics and procedures of travel*: meeting points, food, times of departure and return, money needed, clothing;
- *educational processes*: purpose of visit, preparation in class, follow-up afterwards, assignments for pupils, books, paper or pens needed, photography, video or tape recording.

This would involve a large number of key pieces of information. If delivered as a sustained lecture, packed with detail, much would be forgotten. Feedback becomes, therefore, an important part of the explanation, which, in this particular case, might have to take place in bite-sized chunks, with checks to see that the main points have been absorbed. Thus the teacher might ask, 'Why do you think it's worth going to look at Exmouth?' or 'What sort of interesting things do you think we'll see when we visit the coast?' This would reveal what the children already knew. It would also be wise, indeed essential, to have a prepared page or two of written information with date, cost, times, clothing and food details on it, so that parents would know what is happening. The teacher might having discussed the arrangements, then say, 'Right, turn your papers over and let's see what you can remember. Susan, what time are we leaving?'

Safety aspects might need special consideration, since absolutely everybody must be crystal clear about these, so it would be especially important to check out that every child knew what was needed. (It would be vital to gain attention for this particular matter, otherwise excited children might easily become oblivious to what might seem from their vantage point, a less interesting aspect of the trip.) One teacher has a series of adept ways of gaining attention from excited children on field trips, including, when someone has left a watch, camera or pen lying around, saying something like, 'Who's going to claim this watch before I stamp on it?' The teacher might ask the pupils, 'What safety rules do we need so that no one has an accident or gets lost?' Such matters as cliffs, tides, drowning and road crossing will then emerge, but if they do not, the teacher can put them forward. There might, in the end, be 'Three Golden Rules' for safety, or whatever is appropriate, and the teacher could check that each is understood and remembered. There are numerous ways of obtaining feedback, and the above represents just one set of possibilities out of millions.

Evaluating explanations

Feedback can help with the evaluation of an explanation. It can take the form not only of reactions from pupils or observers to your own teaching, but also knowledge of the results of explanations given by others. This can include research findings, which, although often in generalized form, can sometimes be relevant to individuals. Principally, however, teachers improve their classroom skills by scrutinizing their own strategies and, in the light of feedback, trying out other approaches which might be even more effective. Forms of feedback can include:

Personal feedback

- answers to oral questions;
- written tests of knowledge and understanding;
- children's responses to practical tasks;
- comments and insights of an observer or appraiser;
- listening to a tape or watching a video of your own lesson.

General feedback

- observing and analysing other teachers' or students' explanations;
- watching videos, reading transcripts of other teachers' lessons;
- looking at research findings;
- considering the views of those who have successful experience and expertise, or who are competent to make judgements about effective explaining.

We have already covered a number of these points in the previous five units and the various activities described in them, but soliciting and acting on feedback is such a central matter, it is worthy of as much attention as can sensibly be paid to it. The following section offers examples of possibilities for feedback under each heading.

Answers to oral questions

Consider the following incorrect answers from 10 year olds to an estimation question. They were asked to say roughly how much 8 litres of petrol would cost at 52p a litre. Most pupils correctly estimated it at 'about £4', but three pupils arrived at the figures of £40, £5 and £16 respectively. Further investigation showed the following explanations for the errors:

1 *£40*: A simple place value mistake. The child had multiplied 8 x 5 in her head and blurted out £40 on impulse.

2 *£5*: The teacher had said that 52p was 'a bit over half a pound'. The boy had then surmised that eight halves amounted to four, and the eight 'a bit over' components must be worth another pound.

3 *£16*: The teacher had mentioned, in passing, that petrol was now over £2 a gallon. The pupil had kept this notion in his head and worked out 8 gallons instead of 8 litres.

In each case, the errors and their explanations offer

valuable feedback. The first pupil needs work on place value. The second needs to understand better what estimation involves and that it still needs to be as accurate as possible. The third child's error shows that the teacher needs to think about the confusing effect, to some pupils, of mixing into an explanation about *litres* some information on *gallons,* which mean less to younger generations than to the older adult motorist.

Written tests of knowledge and understanding

Once in a while it is worth making the effort to devote more time to *one particular* written assignment, to see what feedback can be obtained on how effective the explanatory or setting-up phase of the lesson was. For example, if the class has written a piece of imaginative writing, like the 'My Adventure on the Island of Zarg' exercise mentioned earlier in this book on page 32, then a more elaborate than usual marking and grading scheme might be used, looking at such features as: length of story; structure of sentences and whole piece; vocabulary; coherence and organization of story (whether it was easy or hard to follow the story line); which features of the island were mentioned; imaginativeness; grammatical and syntactical accuracy; punctuation and spelling. It is not easy to relate each of these to the teacher's initial explanatory introduction, but it is worth taking note whether children merely reproduced ideas that were mentioned in the interactive or narrative phase of the lesson, or were stimulated to produce their own ideas.

With more factual explanations, a different approach may be necessary. Suppose you have been explaining to a class what insects are. There are several ways in which you can obtain written feedback. For example:

1 *An insect identification sheet* Compile a sheet of ten or twelve pictures of creatures like a butterfly, a house-fly and a cricket (which are insects) and a woodlouse, a spider and a bat (which are not). Ask children to put a tick or cross by each one (see p. 47). Study the errors to see what misconceptions have occurred.

2 *Sentence completion* Draw up a set of sentences with gaps like:
'An insect has (no, two, four, six, eight) legs.'
'Its feelers are on its (body, wings, tail, head).'
'The thorax is in the (middle, front, tail) of an insect.'

Insect identification sheet

Which of these animals are insects?

Put a tick (✓) in the box beside the pictures of insects and a cross (✗) in the box beside the pictures of other sorts of animal.

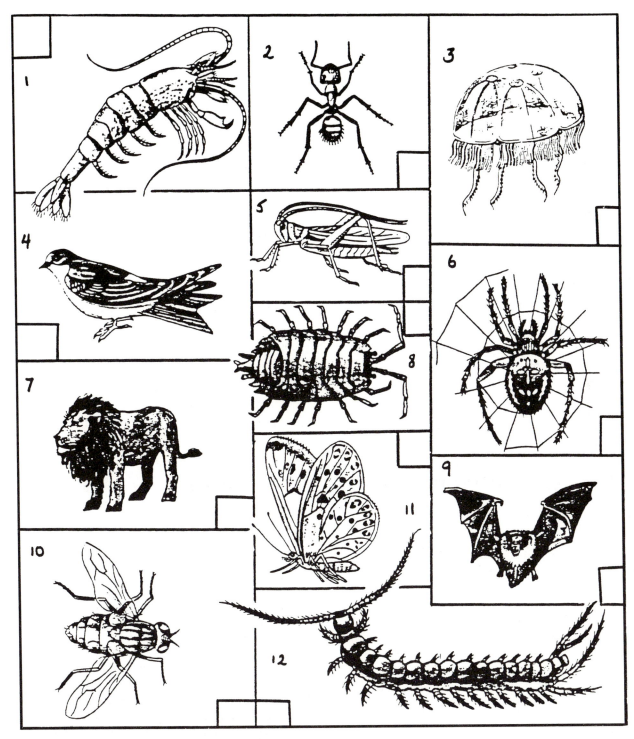

Insect identification sheet

3 *Diagram* Ask the children to draw and label a picture of an insect, putting in the following terms: head, wings, legs, feelers, thorax, abdomen.

4 *Narrative explanation* Give the instructions: 'Peter comes from a country where there are no insects at all. Write a few sentences telling him what insects are.'

Children's responses to a practical task

Try the following activity:

 **ACTIVITY 16**

Discuss with the class what you would need to consider if you were designing something to hold your boiled egg at breakfast time (it need not be an egg *cup*). Decide which design principles you would want to stress.

Give each child access to a range of material – plasticine, empty egg box, middle of kitchen roll, glue, paint, card, etc – which might be used in the design of the egg holder.

Look at the end results. Do the children appear to have grasped and applied the design principles you explained? Did anyone, for example, try to balance an egg on the top of a whole kitchen roll middle and then find he needed most of the glue and plasticine in the school to hold it firm?

Analysing your own or other people's explanations

We have already discussed the analysis of explanations in Unit 3. However, either when an observer is watching you or if you are studying a tape, transcript or video in your own lesson, you can focus on one or more specific aspects and obtain feedback which will help you to improve your skill.

Take, for example, the notion of *opportunity to learn,* that is, children having the chance during a lesson to learn some particular feature. During the Leverhulme Primary Project, we analysed tapes and videos of lessons and compared these with children's responses to test papers. Lists of key concepts were compiled and observers checked each lesson to see if children had had the opportunity to read about, look at, discuss, be told or ask questions about each of these. In many cases where errors

occurred, there had been no detectable *opportunity to learn* in the lesson. If children misconceive, or appear to be confused about some issue or key concept, then replaying a tape or video of a lesson, or discussing it with an observer, may well reveal what caused the confusion or misunderstanding, or, indeed, whether the matter was covered at all.

General feedback – research findings, expert views, pupil views

The findings from research studies can offer, in particular, three useful forms of feedback to the individual teacher. First of all there may be certain general trends that are worth knowing about, though research into teaching and learning does not normally produce the high correlations and huge effect sizes which are found in sciences where the experimenter can exercise tighter control over experimental conditions, such as temperature, volume or pressure, or where inert unchanging substances, rather than human beings, are involved. However, teaching can be improved by small incremental gains, rather than by a single miracle cure-all.

Professor Nate Gage, in his book, *Hard Gains in the Soft Sciences* (1985), tells how relatively trivial experimental effects in medicine can lead to major policy shifts. In 1982 a study was conducted on the effects of a drug called propranolol on patients who had suffered a heart attack. After 30 months, 9.5 per cent of the men who had received a placebo, or dummy pill treatment, had died, whereas only 7 per cent of those given propranolol had died. This difference of 2.5 per cent was regarded as so significant that the experiment was terminated and a general recommendation was made that the new drug should be available to all. Yet, in research on explaining in the classroom, if method A were shown to be only 2.5 per cent superior to method B, no one would dream of suggesting general application. Even slightly significant findings in research on teaching may, therefore, be at least worth considering. Lots of little effects will eventually add up to a much bigger effect.

Second, teachers can try to replicate in their own classrooms, albeit on a modest scale, a study performed elsewhere with several teachers. Activity 17 gives an example of this. Third, even if one is not convinced by findings which may be based on research in different kinds of classroom from one's own, or on research from another country, or with older or younger pupils, or on procedures with which one disagrees, there is often an idea or two

Children making egg holder

which can be taken and adapted to suit one's own conditions. For instance, irrespective of anyone else's findings about the use of rules and examples, an individual teacher can explore her own preferences. She might, therefore, try a pattern of 'rule – example – rule', then one of 'example-rule-example' or even 'example-example-rule'. There is always a way of modifying what someone else has done to suit individual taste. Research findings do not answer all our questions, but they should neither be adulated uncritically, nor dismissed out of hand. Many skilful teachers are, in effect, lifelong researchers into the art and science of their own teaching.

ACTIVITY 17

Applying research in your own classroom

Mary Budd Rowe (1978) investigated the amount of time that teachers allow children to answer a question, known as *wait time*. She analysed 800 tape recordings of lessons and found that teachers often asked between three and five questions per minute, but tended to allow only a second or less for a child to respond before asking someone else, or answering the question themselves, or rephrasing it.

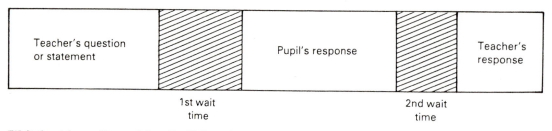

'Wait time' (according to Mary Budd Rowe)

She persuaded teachers to extend the *wait time* to 3 seconds or more, not only after the teacher's question, but also after the child's response, and she found the following results:

1 The length of pupils' responses increased.

2 The number of unsolicited, but appropriate, responses increased.

3 Failure to respond at all decreased.

4 Confidence appeared to increase.

5 The incidence of speculative thinking increased.

6 More child-to-child interaction occurred.

7 Children made more inferences and presented more evidence for what they said.

8 The number of questions asked by children increased.

9 Contributions by slower learning pupils increased.

10 Disciplinary problems decreased.

Try increasing the *wait time* in your own lesson during interactive explanations. Do you get similar results? Or does it create more problems? Not every one of Mary Budd Rowe's results is necessarily beneficial, though many would agree that most seem to have potentially positive effects. By replicating this experiment in your own classroom, see if you learn anything worthwhile. It is advisable to explain to the children that you want to give them more time to answer, so that they see the purpose of what you are doing and feel party to it.

This is not the place to describe in great detail research findings on explaining. The Leverhulme Primary Project research and other related research findings can be found in the two books detailing all the studies carried out during the project, *Primary Teaching Skills* (Wragg 1993) and *Learning to Teach*

(Bennett and Carré 1993). However, it is worth mentioning the seminal work of Smith and Meux (1962) who studied 'episodes' in classrooms and found that explaining was one of the three most common teacher activities, taking about one-eighth of teachers' time. They also found that greatest confusion to children was caused by lack of precision in teachers' questions during explanation.

Brown and Armstrong (1984) found that the most effective (as measured by test scores, pupil and observer ratings) explainers had more keys and more types of keys. They also made more demands on pupils' higher-level thinking. Other researchers quoted by Brown and Armstrong have identified clarity and fluency, emphasis and interest, use of examples, organization and feedback, as elements of explaining which appear to be related to pupil learning.

In the Leverhulme Primary Project we found that when teachers were explaining factual scientific topics, they were more likely to use closed questions, explain links, give or elicit examples, use summaries and visual aids, than when they were explaining more discursive matters. In the latter case, they were more likely to use verbal cues and engage the imagination of pupils. In an experiment where one group of 128 pupils had both factual and discursive topics explained to them and a parallel control group of 128 did *not* have a preliminary explanation, the group that had had an expository phase outperformed the control group both on factual matters and in quality of creative writing, particularly on length, coherence and imaginativeness.

Some of the factors mentioned above apply not only to research findings, but also to the views of those with successful experience. It is always problematic deciding who is or is not arguably 'successful' at explaining, but one often comes across teachers who are regarded as effective communicators by those in a position to know, especially the children themselves. What works for one expert explainer will not necessarily work for another, but none the less advice from experienced practitioners is well worth seeking. It can always be discarded if it does not work. Soliciting advice, especially on specific matters, is a habit worth cultivating. Only the vain and deluded are beyond advice.

If successful practitioners look dumbstruck when asked how to explain effectively, it may be much more fruitful to ask them specific questions, such as, 'How would you explain how an electrical circuit works to 9 year olds?' or 'What can you do to explain simple multiplication to a slow 7 year old?' or 'How would you explain the lunchtime conventions to a newly arrived 5 year old?' Good practitioners often enjoy explaining their art to others, even if they are modest about it. They probably realize that by explaining, that is, as we said right at the beginning of this book, by giving understanding to others, we can all develop our own understanding and, ultimately, our own professional skills.

REFERENCES

Ausubel, D. P., Novak, J. D. and Hanesian, H. (1978) *Educational Psychology: A Cognitive View*, New York: Holt, Rinehart & Winston.

Bennett, S. N. and Carré, C.G. (1993) *Learning to Teach*, London: Routledge.

Bloom, B. S. (ed.) (1956) *Taxonomy of Educational Objectives: Cognitive Domain*, New York: David McKay.

Brown, G. A. (1968) *Microteaching: A Programme of Teaching Skills*, London: Methuen.

Brown, G. A. and Armstrong, S. (1984) 'Explaining and explanations' in Wragg, E. C. (ed.) *Classroom Teaching Skills*, London: Croom Helm.

Brown, G. A. and Wragg, E. C. (1993) *Questioning*, Windsor: NFER-Nelson.

Bruner, J. S. (1966) *Toward a Theory of Instruction*, Cambridge, Mass.: Harvard University Press.

Dunkin, M. J. and Biddle, B. J. (1974) *The Study of Teaching*, New York: Holt, Rinehart & Winston.

Dunne, E. and Bennett, S. N. (1990) *Talking and Learning in Groups*, Basingstoke: Macmillan.

Gage, N. L. (1968) *Explorations of the Teacher's Effectiveness in Explaining*, Stanford University.

Gage, N. L. (1985) *Hard Gains in the Soft Sciences*, Bloomington, Ind.: Phi Delta Kappa.

Harrison, C. (1980) *Readability in the Classroom*, Cambridge: Cambridge University Press.

Piaget, J. (1954) *The Construction of Reality in the Child*, New York: Basic Books.

Rowe, M. B. (1978) *Teaching Science as Continuous Enquiry*, New York: McGraw-Hill.

Smith, B. O. and Meux, M. O. (1962) *A Study of the Logic of Teaching*, Urbana: University of Illinois Press.

Taba, H. (1966) *Teaching Strategies and Cognitive Functioning in Elementary School Children*, USOE Cooperative Research Project No. 1574, San Francisco: San Francisco State College.

Wragg, E. C. (ed.) (1984) *Classroom Teaching Skills*, London: Croom Helm.

——(1993) *Class Management*, Windsor: NFER-Nelson.

——(1993) *Primary Teaching Skills*, London: Routledge.